25 Bicycle Tours in & around Washington, D.C.

D0728209

25 Bicycle Tours in & around Washington, D.C.

ANNE H. OMAN

Photographs by the author
and by Caroline A. Oman

From National
Monuments to
Country Roads

Third Edition

THE COUNTRYMAN PRESS
WOODSTOCK, VERMONT

An Invitation to the Reader
Although it is unlikely that the roads you cycle on these tours will change much with time, some road signs, landmarks, and other terms may. If you find that changes have occurred on these routes, please let us know so we may correct them in future editions. Address all correspondence to:

Editor
The Countryman Press
Bicycling Guides
P.O. Box 748
Woodstock, VT 05091

Copyright © 1991, 1998, and 2006 by Anne H. Oman

Third Edition

All rights reserved. No part of this book may be reproduced in any form or by any electronic or mechanical means, including information storage and retrieval systems, without permission in writing from the publisher, except by a reviewer, who may quote brief passages.

Library of Congress Cataloging-in-Publication Data
Data are available.

ISBN 10: 0-88150-698-2
ISBN 13: 978-0-88150-698-3

Published by The Countryman Press, PO Box 748, Woodstock, VT 05091

Distributed by W. W. Norton & Company, Inc., 500 Fifth Avenue, New York, NY 10110

Text and cover design by Bodenweber Design
Composition by Susan Livingston
Cover photograph by Dennis Coello
Maps by XNR Productions, © The Countryman Press
Interior photographs by the author and by Caroline A. Oman

Printed in the United States of America

10 9 8 7 6 5 4 3

ACKNOWLEDGMENTS I'd like to thank all of the people who went on these tours with me, especially my family, the Gourleys, the Martins, the Joelsons, Dwayne Poston, Erik Smith, Joslin Frank, Lynn Newbury, Hubert Shaiyen, Christian Buhl, Betsy Agle, Charlene van Dijk, Barbara Braucht, Patsy Coffey, Karen Currie, Lorne Lassiter, Gary Ferraro, and Nick Braucht. They endured rain, wrong turns, and other tribulations in the interest of research for this book. I would also like to thank Carl Taylor, who inspired and encouraged me to undertake this project.

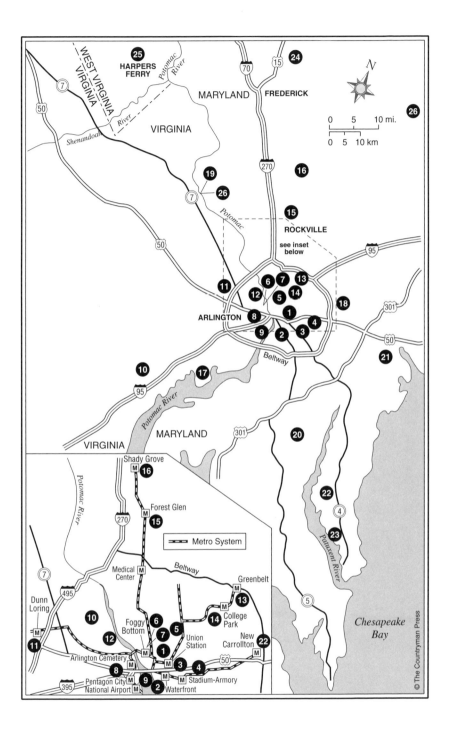

CONTENTS

Note: ⓜ denotes that the tour can be started and finished at a Metro station.

TOURS AT A GLANCE

RIDE	REGION	METRO STATION
1. Museums, Monuments, and Other Major Sights	NW DC	Union Station
2. Washington's Other River	SW, SE, and NE DC	Waterfront/SEU
3. The National Arboretum	NE DC	Stadium-Armory
4. Tenleytown Trot	NW DC	Tenleytown, Foggy Bottom
5. Brookland Bike-About	NE DC	Brookland/CUA
6. The Bicycle Beltway	NW DC and Montgomery County, MD	Foggy Bottom
7. Six-Trail Mix	NW DC and Montgomery County, MD	Foggy Bottom
8. Cycling through Arlington's History	Arlington County, VA	Pentagon City, East Falls Church
9. Along the Potomac to Mount Vernon	Northern Virginia	Ronald Reagan National Airport
10. Lapping Burke Lake	Fairfax County, VA	
11. A Great Ride to Great Falls	Fairfax County, VA	Dunn Loring
12. A Virginia Triangle	Arlington County and Alexandria, VA	Arlington Cemetery

DISTANCE	DIFFICULTY	HIGHLIGHTS
10.3 miles	Easy to moderate; flat except one steep hill	National Mall with museums and memorials, Georgetown, Embassy Row, Washington Cathedral
12.5 miles	Easy; mostly flat	Maine Avenue Fish Market, Titanic Memorial, Navy Museum, Anacostia River banks
5 miles	Moderate; rolling hills	Old Capitol columns, National Bonsai Collection, Mount Hamilton, Asian garden, delightful sampling of trees
8.4 miles	Easy; downhill or flat	Pleasant upscale neighborhoods, Potomac River views, Georgetown waterfront
8.3 miles	Moderate; some hills	National Shrine of the Immaculate Conception, Pope John Paul II Cultural Center, Rock Creek Cemetery, Franciscan Monastery
21.4 miles	Easy to moderate; mostly flat	Georgetown waterfront, Potomac River, Fletcher's Boat House, Bethesda restaurants, Rock Creek Park
33.4 miles	Moderate; mainly flat with a few short uphill climbs	C&O Canal towpath with locks and lock houses, Old Angler's Inn, Glen Echo Park, Clara Barton House
23.6 miles	Moderate; flat and rolling with a few hills	Arlington Historical Museum, Ball-Sellers House, Bon Air Rose Garden, District of Columbia boundary stones, Arlington National Cemetery
28.8 miles	Easy to moderate; paved bike path with a few hills	Potomac River views, Old Town Alexandria, Dyke Marsh, River Farm, Mount Vernon
7.1 miles	Easy; gently rolling paved bike path with one steep hill	Bucolic Burke Lake with many coves and indentations
36 miles	Moderate to difficult; hilly	Great Falls of the Potomac, Riverbend Park, Reston
16.2 miles	Easy to moderate; gradual uphill climbs at start, then downhill or flat	Bluemont Park, Four Mile Run, Ronald Reagan National Airport

DISTANCE	DIFFICULTY	HIGHLIGHTS
14.4 miles	Moderate; hilly in the Beltsville Agricultural Research Center, almost flat in Greenbelt	Country roads, New Deal community of Greenbelt with its art modern architecture
18.5 miles	Easy to moderate; flat with one steep hill	Bladensburg Waterfront Park, Adelphi Mill, University of Maryland, College Park Airport and Aviation Museum
33.2 miles	Moderate to difficult; hilly on roads, flat on bike path	Brookside Gardens, Olney Ale House, Rock Creek Park, Forest Glen Annex with eccentric architecture
44 miles	Moderate to difficult; hilly	Historic Brookeville, Brighton Dam, Triadelphia Reservoir
18.6 miles	Easy to moderate; some hills	Old Pohick Church, Gunston Hall, Mason Neck State Park
11.6 miles	Easy; flat	Wooded rail trail, Marietta Manor Historic Site
77.6 miles	Difficult; hilly	Vineyards, historic towns of Waterford, Middleburg, Leesburg
28.5 miles	Easy to moderate; almost flat	Patuxent River Park, Merkle Wildlife Sanctuary, St. Thomas Church
51.4 miles	Moderate; rolling to moderately hilly	Historic churches, Old Quaker Burying Ground, Galesville waterfront
12.4 miles	Easy to moderate; stretches	St. Ignatius Church, Port Tobacco Chapel Point State Park, Port Tobacco courthouse, Thomas Stone Historic Site
17.4 or 34.8 miles	Moderate to difficult; some hills	Jefferson Patterson Park, Battle Creek Cypress Swamp, historic Benedict
24.6 miles	Moderate; some hills	Three covered bridges, Catoctin Furnace, Cozy Inn
54 or 102.6 miles	Moderate to difficult; rolling or flat with a few steep hills	Jubal A. Early ferry, historic Leesburg and Harpers Ferry
41.1 or 82.2 miles	Moderate; one short climb, then flat	Gunpowder Falls, historic rail stations with museums, Mason-Dixon Line marker, Howard Tunnel, historic York

INTRODUCTION   Washington is a big, booming metropolis, but a great place to bike. A system of trails, a disproportionate number of national and local parks, a subway system accessible to cyclists at certain times, and a network of activist cyclists who lobby for better bicycling conditions all combine to make the Washington area hospitable to two-wheeled touring. The Washington area also has an amazing variety of natural and built attractions—from the Great Falls of the Potomac to the Washington Cathedral, from the tidewaters of the Chesapeake Bay to the Civil War town of Harpers Ferry.

ABOUT THE RIDES   The tours in this book are designed to take the rider to well-known and lesser-known places within the city of Washington and its suburbs—and to facilitate getaways to rural areas surprisingly close to the city. The rides will appeal most to people who like to combine cycling with visiting historic and scenic points of interest.

There are rides in this book to suit just about every level of cycling ability and every time frame. A short ride around the National Arboretum makes a nice family activity on a Sunday afternoon. The trip to Harpers Ferry is ideal for a weekend, and the trip to Waterford and Middleburg could be stretched to three days or completed in two. Most of the trips can easily be completed in one day—but some can be stretched into overnight trips if schedules permit. The people who made the trips with me ranged in age from 7 to 60-plus. You can set your own pace on these tours. If you have children or people unused to cycling in your party, you'll want to take more rest stops and allow extra time to walk up some hills.

Because different cyclists set different paces, I haven't tried to estimate the time necessary to complete a tour. You can spend all day on a

10-mile tour if you stop often to rest, picnic, swim, and see the sights. On the other hand, you can easily ride 40 to 50 miles in less than a day. I found 25 miles to be a good distance for a one-day tour—challenging enough but allowing time for poking around old cemeteries or wading in streams. I've tried to avoid backtracking, but sometimes this wasn't possible.

ABOUT THE METRO Many of the tours start from Metrorail stations. Bicyclists are allowed to bring their bikes on the trains anytime except rush hours (7–10 AM and 4–7 PM) on weekdays, and at any time on weekends and most federal holidays (except major crowd events, such as the Independence Day Celebration). Permits are no longer required. Bicyclists may use any car on the train and enter it through either the first or last doors, not the middle door. The number of bikes per train is limited. Using the Metro is great because it gets you nearer to your destination without the bother and expense of car bike racks. Call 202-962-1116 for more information and to make sure the current policy is still operative. Even if you don't want to take a train, you might want to park at one of the station parking lots, which are free on weekends (though not all stations have them). For more information about parking at Metro stations, call 202-637-7000.

ABOUT SAFETY Cycling in a metropolitan area involves two kinds of safety considerations. A cyclist needs to protect himself or herself from criminal activity as well as from traffic hazards. The tours in this book are all in areas considered safe, in daylight hours, at the time of publication. But "safe" is a relative term, and no place is completely without danger. Prudent cyclists will use common sense to protect themselves and their bikes against crime and other dangers. Here are some important safety tips:

- Never ride alone, particularly on a secluded trail or road.
- Always let someone know what route you are taking.
- Don't ride after dark.
- Carry a whistle around your neck or an air horn in an accessible pocket. Noise can both bring help and scare away attackers.
- Ride with the traffic flow. This is a legal requirement.
- Wear a helmet (see "About Equipment").

Burke Lake Park provides a bucolic oasis in Northern Virginia's suburban sprawl.

Cyclists admire Washington's cherry blossoms, which surround the Jefferson Memorial.

- Use hand signals before turning. A left arm out straight signals a left turn. A left arm bent upward at a right angle signals a right turn. A left arm bent downward at a right angle signals slowing or stopping.
- When riding with companions, ride single file at least 20 feet apart.

- Don't wear headsets or ear plugs.
- Be sure your bicycle is in good working order.
- Watch out for storm drains, potholes, railroad or trolley tracks, patches of sand or gravel, and other road hazards.
- Ride defensively. Cars are bigger than you are. Watch for people opening the doors of parked cars on your side of the road.
- Pull well away from the road when you stop to rest or check the map.

BIKE SECURITY Always secure your bike when you leave it—even for a few minutes. This is especially important in urban areas, where bicycle theft is a serious problem. In addition:

- Lock your bike to something permanent and in a place where any attempted theft is likely to be noticed.
- Lock up as much of your bike as possible. If you have quick-release wheels, remove the front wheel and put the lock through the front wheel, the rear wheel, and the frame, securing it to the rack, tree, or other fixture. Remove any accessories you don't want to lose— pumps, water bottles, and odometers are vulnerable to theft.
- Register your bike with your local police department. This will greatly enhance your chances of getting it back if it's stolen.

ABOUT EQUIPMENT All you really need are a touring or mountain bike in good condition, a helmet, a lock (see above), and clothing suitable for the weather. The Washington Area Bicyclist Association (WABA) publishes *A Consumer's Guide to Bicycle Helmets*. To obtain a copy, call 202-944-8567.

Other useful equipment includes a patch kit and spare tube, a bike-mounted air pump, a bike-mounted water bottle, a rear-view mirror attached either to your helmet or to your handlebars, an odometer (either the computer type that is installed on your handlebars or the less expensive mechanical variety that attaches on your front wheel), and some kind of carrying device. Packs that attach to your bike are more comfortable than backpacks.

BIKE RENTALS Many bicycle shops rent bikes, racks, child carriers, helmets, and other equipment. If you want to rent a bike for a particular tour, call the bike shop listed at the end of the tour. In addition, rental bikes are available at Fletcher's Boat House (202-244-0461) on the Chesapeake & Ohio Canal at Thompson Boat Center (202-333-4861), convenient to the C&O Canal Trail, the Rock Creek Trail, and D.C. monuments, and at Bike the Sites (202-966-8662) in the Old Post Office Pavilion at Pennsylvania Avenue and 12th Street NW near the Federal Triangle Metro station.

SOURCES FOR MAPS AND OTHER INFORMATION   Maps in this book are designed to provide all the information bicyclists taking these tours will need. However, you can obtain additional maps and tips from the various political jurisdictions—states, counties, etc. An easier method is to send a self-addressed, stamped envelope to the Washington Area Bicyclist Association (WABA) and ask for a list of maps and other guides. WABA will send you an order form and will fill your request promptly. You may also visit the association's shop to purchase your maps: 1015 31st Street NW, Washington D.C. 20007-4406 (202-944-8567).

ORGANIZED CYCLING   Several organizations in the Washington area run frequent group cycling trips. Foremost among these are the following:

Potomac Pedalers Touring Club. Each weekend, the Potomac Pedalers run a dozen or more trips for cyclists of varying abilities. The group rates each ride according to seven categories, which range from "Casual" (from 5 to 15 miles in length), to "Fast Training" (for race-oriented cyclists). Nonmembers are welcome on the rides, but it's difficult to find out about them if you're not a member. The schedule is published in the club newsletter, Pedal Patter, which is mailed to members and is also available at some bicycle shops. Each ride has a leader, whose phone number is listed in the newsletter description in case a reader needs more information. There are no charges for the rides. For membership information, call 202-363-TOUR or go to www.bikepptc.org.

Bike the Sites, Inc., offers professionally guided bike tours to various tourist attractions, including Mount Vernon. The fee includes a bicycle and helmet. Call 202-966-8662 for more information or go to www .bikethesites.com.

In addition, other groups offer rides on an occasional basis. Check for "Cycling" in the sports listings in Friday's "Weekend" section of the *Washington Post*.

CITY AND SUBURBS

Reflected in the pool at the bottom of Capitol Hill, the Botanical Garden provides a backdrop for cyclists.

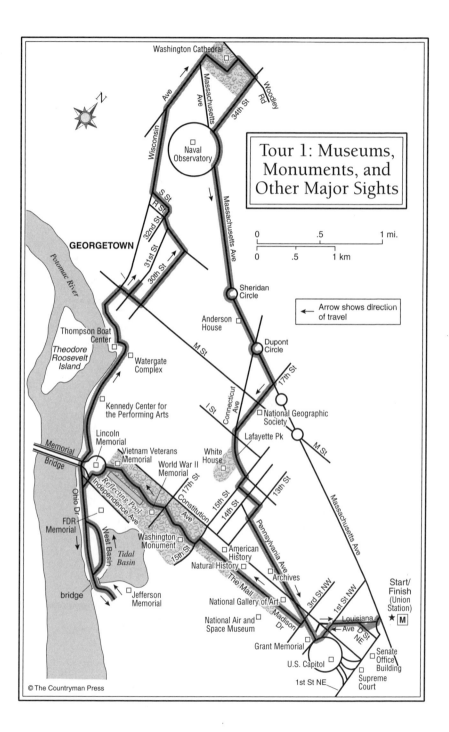

Tour 1: Museums, Monuments, and Other Major Sights

Washington Cathedral

Washington Cathedral

Massachusetts Ave

Ave

Woodley Rd

34th St

Wisconsin

Naval Observatory

S St

R St

32nd St

31st St

30th St

GEORGETOWN

Potomac River

Massachusetts Ave

0   .5   1 mi.
0   .5   1 km

Sheridan Circle

Arrow shows direction of travel

Anderson House

M St

Dupont Circle

Thompson Boat Center

Theodore Roosevelt Island

Watergate Complex

17th St

Kennedy Center for the Performing Arts

1 St

Connecticut Ave

National Geographic Society

M St

Lincoln Memorial

Lafayette Pk

White House

Memorial Bridge

Vietnam Veterans Memorial

World War II Memorial

17th St

15th St

14th St

13th St

Pennsylvania Ave

Massachusetts Ave

Ohio Dr

Reflecting Pool

Independence Ave

Constitution Ave

FDR Memorial

West Basin

Washington Monument

15th St

American History

Archives

3rd St NW

1st St NW

Start/Finish (Union Station)

★ M

Tidal Basin

Natural History

The Mall

Louisiana

bridge

Jefferson Memorial

National Gallery of Art

Madison Dr

Ave

D St NE

1st St NE

Senate Office Building

National Air and Space Museum

Grant Memorial

U.S. Capitol

Supreme Court

1st St NE

© The Countryman Press

1

Museums, Monuments, and Other Major Sights

LOCATION: District of Columbia

METRO ACCESS: Union Station

TERRAIN: One fairly steep uphill climb, otherwise flat with only a few moderate hills

ROAD CONDITIONS: Bike paths and some city streets with light traffic on weekends

DISTANCE: 10.3 miles

HIGHLIGHTS: Washington's major monuments and museums plus Georgetown, Embassy Row, the White House

This is a great tour if you're a newcomer to Washington or if you want to show visitors your city from a different perspective. (To find out where you can rent bikes for visitors, see the introduction.) While it will take only a couple of hours to breeze by all these attractions, you can easily spend all day on this tour if you actually visit the sights. Be sure to bring good bike locks.

Start your tour at Union Station, either at the Metro stop or in the pay parking lot. Be sure to take time either before or after the tour to explore the station building, which is loosely modeled on Rome's Baths of Caracalla. Still in use as a major train station, it also holds shops, restaurants, food stands, and nine movie theaters.

0.0 Cross Massachusetts Avenue in the pedestrian crosswalk in front of the Christopher Columbus fountain and follow the diagonal sidewalk path to the right, across a small park.

0.2 Cross D Street NE and follow the sidewalk to the right, past a pool and fountains with a view of the Capitol in the background. Turn left on Louisiana Avenue NW.

0.4 Turn left onto First Street NW and continue until you are in front of the Capitol. Cross the street and use the curb cut to walk your bike onto the sidewalk in front of the Grant Memorial.

Self-taught sculptor Henry M. Shrady won a hard-fought commission to design a memorial to the Civil War hero and president. It includes an equestrian statue and almost disturbingly realistic war scenes.

0.6 After your visit, bike around the north rim of the Capitol Reflecting Pool. Cross Third Street NW and enter Madison Drive, which parallels the Mall on the north side.

1.0 The National Gallery of Art is on your right.

It includes the angular I.M. Pei East Wing—which houses Calder mobiles, Joan Miró tapestries, and changing exhibits, the classical West Wing, home to paintings ranging from the Renaissance to the 20th century, and an outdoor sculpture garden. There's a bike rack at the east entrance to the West Wing.

Continue along Madison Drive, stopping to visit museums and other attractions at will.

1.1 The National Air and Space Museum is on the left across the Mall.

The National Archives, repository of the Constitution and the Declaration of Independence, is on your right across Constitution Avenue.

1.2 The National Museum of Natural History is on your right.

It houses the Hope diamond, an insect zoo, dinosaur skeletons, and millions of other artifacts. Across the Mall is the Smithsonian "Castle," which holds the tomb of James Smithson. The scholarly, illegitimate son of an English lord, Smithson left his fortune to establish in the United States an institution devoted to knowledge, even though he never visited this country. Adjacent to the castle is a carousel.

1.3 Across the Mall is a complex of underground museums devoted to Asian, African, and Pacific Island art.

Adjacent to this complex is the aboveground Freer Gallery, with a fine collection of Asian

*art plus representative paintings by Winslow Homer, James Whistler, and others. A high-
light is the "Peacock" dining room designed and decorated by Whistler.*

1.4 Park your bike in the rack in front of the National Museum of American
History and browse through the eclectic collection.

*It includes the inaugural ball gowns of all the First Ladies, the red slippers from the movie
The Wizard of Oz, and the original flag that inspired Francis Scott Key to write "The
Star-Spangled Banner." The Mall ends here, at 14th Street, but Madison Drive continues
one more block to 15th Street.*

1.6 Cross 15th Street in the pedestrian crossing and ride up the hill to the
Washington Monument.

*Even if you don't want to wait in line long enough to ascend, you'll have a fine view of the
Lincoln Memorial and the Reflecting Pool ahead of you and of the White House to your
right.*

Take the path that veers off to your right and follow it to the crosswalk across
17th Street.

1.9 Walk your bike across 17th Street in the crosswalk and admire the World
War II Memorial.

*The massive monument, opened in April 2004, honors the 16 million men and women
who served in the U.S. armed forces during World War II.*

After your visit, walk your bike behind the memorial and to the right and enter
the wide, hard-packed dirt trail that runs beside the Reflecting Pool.

The pool was modeled on those leading to the palace at Versailles and to the Taj Mahal.

2.2 Lock your bike in the rack near the information kiosk and visit the Lincoln
Memorial, the Korean War Memorial, and the Vietnam Veterans Memorial.

*There are restrooms under the Lincoln Memorial. If you visit them, you can also view the
stalactites growing under the monument.*

Follow the sidewalk to your left around the memorial and cross Independence
Avenue near the Ericsson Memorial, dedicated to the inventor of the screw
propeller. Cross Ohio Drive and enter the bike path, heading left.

*You may want to rest under the willows on the banks of the Potomac and gaze over at
Arlington House, home of Robert E. Lee, on the Virginia side.*

2.6 Turn left into the Franklin Delano Roosevelt Memorial.

Built of red South Dakota granite and resplendent with waterfalls and realistic bronze sculpture, the memorial was designed by Lawrence Halprin. FDR in a flowing cape with his dog Fala by his side is one of the most popular attractions. The Depression figures— including an urban breadline, a rural couple, and a man pressed to an old-fashioned radio listening to a "fireside chat"—are by noted sculptor George Segal.

3.0 Exit the last of the outdoor "rooms" that make up the FDR Memorial and follow the paved path across the grass toward the bridge. Cross the bridge over the Tidal Basin.

Observe the fish-tailed gargoyles on the bridge. They were added in 1987, and their faces are portraits of former National Park Service director, Jack Fish.

As soon as you've crossed the bridge, bear left to the Jefferson Memorial. After visiting the memorial, double back across the bridge and take West Basin Drive to your right.

This will lead you past the famous cherry trees, a gift from Japan.

3.6 At the fork, bear left, following the signs toward the Lincoln Memorial. Cross Ohio Drive and re-enter the bike path, heading right.

3.9 Pass under Memorial Bridge, where the path narrows. Walk your bike.

4.0 The Watergate Steps, which preceded the famous apartment complex by several decades, served as a ceremonial entry to Washington for VIPs arriving by sea.

Later, but before airplane and road noise precluded the idea, the steps were the site of concerts. Old-movie buffs may remember that Sophia Loren skipped out of a concert here to begin her romance with Cary Grant in Houseboat.

4.6 On your right is the Kennedy Center for the Performing Arts and, just beyond it, the Watergate complex.

4.8 Turn left to the Thompson Boat Center (bike and boat rentals available); then bear right and walk your bike on the brick sidewalk that leads along the newly renovated Georgetown waterfront.

You'll pass fountains, outdoor cafés, and a realistic sculpture of a man in a turtleneck and cap filling his pipe. Across the river (left) lies Theodore Roosevelt Island, a nature preserve. You'll probably see crews and individuals rowing on the river.

Cyclists pause at the reflecting pool between the Washington Monument and the Lincoln Memorial.

4.9 Turn right, exit the waterfront complex, cross K Street NW, and enter Wisconsin Avenue, riding uphill.

5.0 Cross a bridge over the C&O Canal (see Tour 7). Continue up Wisconsin to M Street and turn right.

Watch for heavy traffic in the heart of the Georgetown commercial area.

5.1 Cross M Street at 31st in the pedestrian crosswalk and walk your bike to the Old Stone House at 3051 M Street NW.

Built in 1765, the oldest surviving residential structure in the city is open for tours Wednesday through Sunday. It was the home of a cabinetmaker and his family and provides a rare glimpse of what life was like for the middle class in the 18th century. The garden in back is a great place for picnics, and carryout food is available at several places on M Street.

Continue east on M Street to 30th Street; then turn left up 30th Street through the fashionable 19th-century Georgetown residential district.

5.5 Turn left onto R Street, skirting Oak Hill Cemetery and Montrose Park (right).

At 31st and R Streets is the entrance to Dumbarton Oaks Gardens, containing formal and informal gardens and fountains and an "orangerie." The gardens are open 2–6 PM daily, and there is an admission charge.

5.6 Turn right onto 32nd Street.

The Dumbarton Oaks Museum, including the house where the representatives from major powers met to lay the foundation for the United Nations, the pre-Columbian collection, and the Byzantine collection, is located at 1703 32nd Street. It's open Tuesday through Sunday 2–5 PM, and a donation is suggested.

5.7 Turn left onto S Street, then right onto Wisconsin Avenue. Be prepared for heavy traffic and a steep climb.

6.4 On your left is the Soviet Embassy's residential and office complex on a site known as Mount Alto.

Before glasnost, a great brouhaha developed when it was discovered that, from this elevated site, the Soviets could intercept secret signals.

6.6 Turn right onto South Road on the Washington Cathedral grounds.

This Gothic cathedral, in the style of 14th-century English ecclesiastical architecture, was begun in 1907 and completed in 1990. Volunteers give tours and point out the moon rock incorporated into a stained-glass window, the crypt of Woodrow Wilson (the only president buried in the District of Columbia), and other features. An elevator takes visitors to the Pilgrim Gallery for a spectacular view from one of Washington's highest points.

After visiting the cathedral, take the road to the right of the building, past the peaceful Bishop's Garden. Bear right at the nursery and exit the cathedral grounds at Woodley Road NW.

6.8 Turn right onto Woodley Road.

6.9 Turn right onto 34th Street. Watch for heavy traffic.

7.4 Turn left onto Massachusetts Avenue NW.

As soon as you make the turn, you'll see the U.S. Naval Observatory on your right. You may enter only if you go on one of the 90-minute tours, which are held weekdays at 12:30 and 2 PM. On the grounds is the vice president's house, which is not open to the public.

7.7 The British Embassy complex is on your right.

It includes a modern office building that was added onto the residence designed by Sir Edwin Lutyens, architect of many of the great country houses of England. In front of the residence, with one foot on the embassy's British soil and one foot on American soil, is a statue of Winston Churchill, cigar in hand.

7.8 The Embassies of Bolivia and Brazil are on the right.

7.9 The Islamic Center and Mosque is on your left.

The complex was built with monetary and material contributions from many Muslim countries. Note that it does not face the street exactly—it faces Mecca. Non-Muslim visitors are welcome. You must remove your shoes before entering.

8.0 The Embassy of Japan is on your right; the Embassy of Venezuela is on your left.

8.2 The United Arab Emirates Embassy is on your right.

The limestone chateau across the avenue, designed in 1906 by local architect George Oakley Totten, serves as the Embassy of Cameroon.

8.3 Yield to traffic in Sheridan Circle, which contains a statue of General Sheridan on his horse, Rienzi.

The work is nicknamed "an officer and a gentleman." On your right is the Embassy of Turkey.

8.4 Anderson House is on your right.

The house contains a museum of artifacts of the Society of the Cincinnati, an organization of descendants of George Washington's officers, and a lovely garden. It's open for tours afternoons Tuesday through Saturday.

8.5 The Embassy of Indonesia is on your right.

The embassy occupies the former home of Evalyn Walsh McLean, whose father struck it rich in the Colorado goldfields and who owned the Hope diamond.

Continue on Massachusetts Avenue through Dupont Circle.

8.8 Turn right onto 17th Street NW and continue to the intersection of 17th and M Streets.

Lock your bike to a tree or sign and visit Explorers Hall of the National Geographic Society. It's open daily and the changing exhibits are free.

Continue south on 17th Street.

9.2 At I Street, 17th Street intersects with Connecticut Avenue. Bear left onto Connecticut to Lafayette Park.

The square surrounding the park is actually known as Jackson Square, and although there is a statue of Lafayette in the park, the central place is occupied by an equestrian statue of Andrew Jackson, his horse rearing in the direction of the house he once occupied. Washington's elite—including Henry Adams, John Hay, Dolley Madison, and Stephen Decatur—lived on this square. Many of the houses have been preserved and are used as government offices. The Stephen Decatur House, on the northwest corner of the square, is open to the public. You may also visit St. John's, "the Church of the Presidents," at the corner of 16th and H Streets.

Walk your bike through the park to Pennsylvania Avenue for a view of the White House. Turn left and follow Pennsylvania Avenue past the Treasury Building.

9.4 Following the inaugural parade route—but backward—turn right onto 15th Street NW. Just past the Treasury Building, cross at the pedestrian crossing into Pershing Square.

The square contains a memorial to General "Black Jack" Pershing plus an ice-skating rink that turns into a water garden in summer.

Cross 14th Street and enter the Western Plaza, with its fountains and inscriptions about the city.

On your right is the Beaux Arts–style District Building, Washington's city hall.

Walk or ride across the plaza; then cross Pennsylvania Avenue and continue riding down the "avenue of presidents."

9.6 The Old Post Office Building, saved from the wrecking ball in the 1970s, holds shops and restaurants.

There's a great view from the tower. Across Pennsylvania Avenue is the Hoover Building, FBI headquarters.

9.7 The Navy Memorial and bandstand (left) was undertaken as part of the Pennsylvania Avenue spruce-up.

9.8 Modern and monumental, the Canadian Embassy (left) is the first embassy to be built on Pennsylvania Avenue. Its gallery features works by Canadian artists and is open to the public.

10.0 Pennsylvania Avenue NW ends at the foot of Capitol Hill. Turn left onto First Street NW and follow it past the intersection with Constitution Avenue. Bear right onto Louisiana Avenue.

10.3 Return to the starting point, Union Station.

Bicycle Repair Service

Big Wheel Bikes, 1034 33rd Street NW (202-337-0254)

The Bike Shop at District Hardware, 2003 P Street NW (202-659-8686)

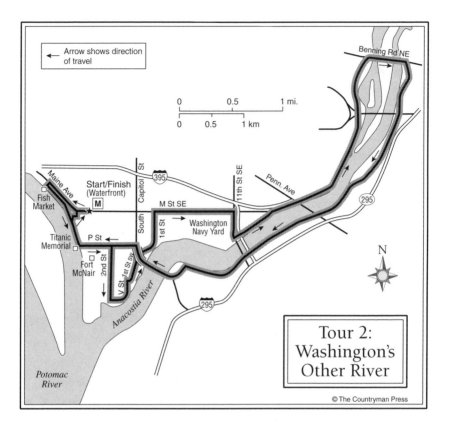

Arrow shows direction of travel

0   0.5   1 mi.
0   0.5   1 km

Benning Rd NE

Maine Ave

Fish Market

Start/Finish (Waterfront)
M

Capitol St

395

11th St SE

Penn. Ave

295

Titanic Memorial

P St

South St

1st St

M St SE

Washington Navy Yard

Fort McNair

2nd St

V St   1st St SW

Anacostia River

295

Potomac River

N

Tour 2:
Washington's
Other River

© The Countryman Press

2

Washington's Other River

LOCATION: The District of Columbia

METRO ACCESS: Waterfront/SEU

TERRAIN: Flat

ROAD CONDITIONS: Paved bike trails, park roads, and city streets

DISTANCE: 12.5 miles

HIGHLIGHTS: The Maine Avenue Fish Market, the Titanic
Memorial, the Washington Navy Yard, the Anacostia River banks.

Although everyone associates Washington with the Potomac
River, the District does have another hometown waterway, the
Anacostia—sometimes just called the Eastern Branch of the Potomac.
Fed by numerous streams, the Anacostia flows 8.4 miles through Prince
George's County, Maryland, and the eastern and southern corners of
the District of Columbia and empties into the larger Potomac at Hains
Point. Like many area rivers, the Anacostia was "discovered" by Captain John Smith, who found thriving villages populated by the Nanchotank tribe along its banks. The Nanchotank word *anaquah,* meaning
"village or trading center," gave the river its name. The Nanchotanks
used the river not only for transportation and commerce but also as a
food source, taking shad, perch, sunfish, catfish, and herring from its
waters. Alas, although you will probably see people fishing along the
river's banks on this tour, the water quality has seriously deteriorated
since Smith's visit. Agricultural development spurred soil erosion and
sedimentation, and urbanization brought pollution as sewage and re-
fuse spilled into the river. Over the past two decades, environmental

groups and local governments have worked together to revitalize the river, improving sewage and drainage systems and restoring wetlands.

Another part of the revitalization effort is a cycling/walking trail that takes in both sides of the Anacostia. Though still a work-in-progress, the trail is well marked with blue and green signs reading "Anacostia Riverwalk Trail." This tour uses the interim trail and it starts and ends either at the Waterfront/SEU station on Metro's Green Line or at the Maine Avenue Fish Market a few blocks away, which has very limited parking—but excellent crab cake sandwiches. Eventually, the River-walk trail will be linked to a 26-mile network of trails along the Anacostia's branches in Maryland (see Tour 14).

0.0 From Waterfront/SEU Metro station, turn right on M Street SW.

0.2 Turn left onto the frontage road, which is called Water Street. Take Water Street to your right, past seafood restaurants and marinas to the Maine Avenue Fish Market.

The fish wharf is all that remains of a much larger working waterfront with wharves, piers, and warehouses. Chesapeake Bay watermen once tied their boats up here and sold fish, crabs, and oysters; today, the seafood arrives by truck. After touring the colorful—and pungent—market, double back along Water Street. The body of water on your right is not the Anacostia but the Washington Channel. Across the channel lies Hains Point, where the Washington Channel, the Anacostia, and the Potomac meet.

0.8 Cross a parking lot and enter a pedestrian/cyclist trail, which leads to the *Titanic* Memorial.

It's not clear whether the pose in the movie of the same name was copied from this statue by Gertrude Vanderbilt Whitney, but it certainly looks that way. The sculpture of the par-tially clad man—in the symbolic form of a cross—is a tribute to the hundreds of male pas-sengers on the Titanic who gave up their places in the lifeboats to women and children. According to James Goode's classic, The Outdoor Sculpture of Washington, D.C., the statue represents self-sacrifice and "the last inspiration of a departing soul." Behind the statue, you can glimpse the homes of high military officers along the Washington Channel on the grounds of Fort McNair.

1.0 Turn left in front of the statue and follow the trail sign along the sidewalk past the brick wall that encloses Fort McNair, home of the National War College.

1.2 Turn right on Second Street SW and left on V Street SW.

The Titanic *Memorial graces the southwest waterfront.*

The Pepco generating plant on your left was the site of the home of one of Washington's first African-American millionaires, Lewis Jefferson. A contractor, real estate developer, shipbuilder, boat captain, and amusement park owner, Jefferson built a large brick house here for his wife and 14 children in 1903. It was demolished in the 1930s for the power plant. Across V Street is a pumping station donated by Pepco to a conservation group. The old pumping station is also the headquarters of DC Sail, which gives sailing lessons to neighborhood children and rents sailboats. (For more information, go to www.dcsail.org.) The pumping house pier provides a sweeping view of the Anacostia River and a vantage point for watching ospreys land.

2.0 Enter the soft-surface trail in front of the old pump house and continue left along the river for 0.1 mile, then re-enter the road, bearing left on Half Street SW.

2.3 Turn right on Water Street.

2.4 Turn right on S Street, then make an immediate left onto South Capitol Street.

2.5 Turn right on Potomac Avenue.

2.7 Turn left on First Street.

You are in an industrial area that will eventually make way for a new baseball stadium.

3.2 Turn right onto M Street SE, which climbs a small hill past the Washington Navy Yard.

Established in 1799 and the Navy's oldest shore facility in continuous use, the Navy Yard has served many purposes in its long history. Originally a shipbuilding facility, the yard became known as the "gun factory" during the Civil War. It is now undergoing still more change as the Navy moves some of its office operations to this facility. During the War of 1812, the yard's commandant, Captain Thomas Tingey, set fire to the facility to keep it out of British hands. Virtually all that remains of the original facility is the ceremonial gate, designed by Capitol architect Benjamin Latrobe in 1805 and now topped by an 1878 addition.

3.7 Turn right onto 11th Street SE and stay in the right lane. When the road turns, enter a gravel path that leads under the 11th Street Bridge.

To your right is the entrance to the Navy Yard's portion of the Anacostia Riverwalk Trail, which leads to the Navy Museum. The museum charts the history of the U.S. Navy from the revolution to the present, and exhibits include gun decks, a submarine room with working periscopes, and historical memorabilia. In Willard Park, in front of the Navy Museum, is an outdoor display of military weapons and hardware, plus a few picnic tables. At the pier is the U.S.S. Barry, a destroyer commissioned in 1956 and now a permanent visit ship at the Navy Yard. The Barry, which saw action in waters off Cuba and Vietnam, is open daily for self-guided tours.

After your tour, backtrack to the gate and continue along the gravel path, past the 11th Street Boathouse. On spring weekends, many local crews compete here. After you pass the boathouse, turn left and exit onto Water Street SE, turning right. The road leads you past several small marinas.

4.8 Where Water Street ends, turn right onto M Street SE and continue along the waterfront and under the John Philip Sousa Bridge. Just past the bridge, dismount and carry your bike across the railroad tracks to the left and enter the RFK Stadium Road, which can be used by cars only when there's an event at the stadium. Turn right.

On your left, over the trees, you can see some of the granite and marble monuments in Congressional Cemetery, Washington's official burying ground until Arlington Cemetery was built after the Civil War and final resting place of the aforesaid John Philip Sousa and others.

6.2 The road enters a series of stadium parking lots. Continue through the parking lots along the river.

To your left is a farmers' market, where fresh produce is sold from trucks. To your right is a footbridge leading to two small islands in the river, Kingman Island and Heritage Island. Both feature nature trails.

6.6 Exit the parking lot onto busy Benning Road NE, turn right, and continue over a bridge to the other side of the Anacostia. At the end of the bridge, turn right onto the paved River Terrace Trail, which leads through a park with a gazebo. At the end of the park, the paved trail turns into a dirt service road, which leads through woods and fields and ends at some railroad tracks. Carry your bike across the tracks and turn right, continuing through Anacostia Park.

The park is used for picnics and soccer games and for viewing the boat races on the river.

10.3 Bear left toward the Frederick Douglass Bridge, then take the trail under the bridge, which leads to the pedestrian walkway. Cross the bridge on the narrow walkway and continue on the service road along South Capitol Street SW.

11.3 Turn left onto P Street SW and continue past Fort McNair onto the sidewalk trail that leads to the Titanic Memorial.

11.9 Turn right at the memorial and continue to the parking lot. Exit onto M Street SE and turn right.

12.5 Cross M Street at the signal and enter the Waterfront/SEU Metro station.

Bicycle Repair Service

Capitol Hill Bikes, 709 8th Street SE (202-544-4234)

The National Arboretum

LOCATION: The northeast quadrant of the District of Columbia

TERRAIN: Rolling hills

ROAD CONDITIONS: Paved roads with light traffic

DISTANCE: 5 miles

HIGHLIGHTS: A delightful sampling of gardens, trees, and views

The main purpose of the 444-acre National Arboretum is to facilitate government research on trees, shrubs, and herbaceous plants, but it's also a boon to bicyclists who want to take a short, refreshing country ride without leaving the city. You can stop and look at everything or just breeze on through, smelling the blossoms as you pass. Here's a rough idea of what you'll smell—and see—and when:

Late March–mid-April: Daffodils, magnolias, camellias, quince, rhododendrons, flowering cherries, crab apples

Late April–May: Azaleas, dogwoods, mountain laurel, peonies, old roses, wildflowers, lilacs

June–August: Day lilies, lilies, waterlilies, crape myrtles, herbs

September–October: Deciduous trees in their fall color show; even the dwarf trees in the Bonsai Collection

To get to the National Arboretum from downtown Washington, take New York Avenue east to Bladensburg Road NE. Turn right on Bladensburg, then left onto R Street NE to the entrance. There is a large parking lot.

0.0 Exit the parking lot and turn right onto Azalea Road.

0.2 Turn left onto Mount Hamilton Road.

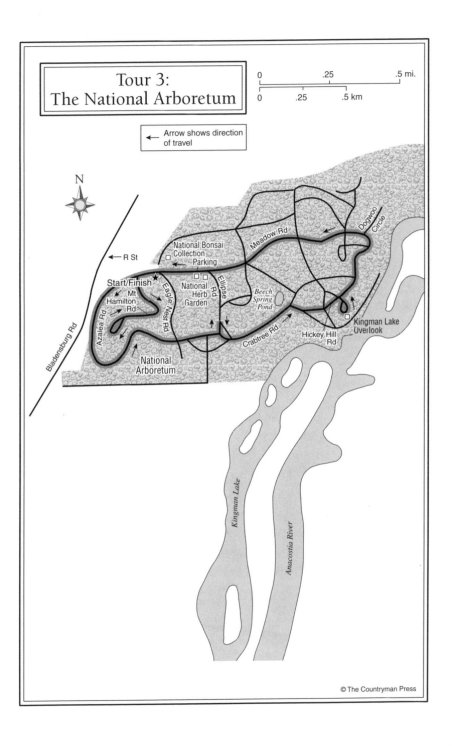

Tour 3:
The National Arboretum

0   .25   .5 mi.

0   .25   .5 km

← Arrow shows direction
of travel

N

← R St

National Bonsai
Collection
Parking

Meadow Rd

Dogwood Circle

Start/Finish

Mt
Hamilton
Rd

Eagle Nest Rd

National
Herb
Garden

Ellipse Rd

Beech
Spring
Pond

Azalea Rd

National
Arboretum

Crabtree Rd

Hickey Hill
Rd

Kingman Lake
Overlook

Bladensburg Rd

Kingman Lake

Anacostia River

© The Countryman Press

This road winds up through azaleas, rhododendrons, and may apples to the top of 239-foot Mount Hamilton. Rest on the bench at the top of the "mountain" and drink in the view of the Capitol, the Library of Congress, the Washington Monument, the Washington Cathedral, and the Shrine of the Immaculate Conception.

0.6 Proceed down the mountain and back to Azalea Road.

1.0 Go left onto Azalea Road.

On your left you'll see azalea-strewn Mount Hamilton; on your right, crab apple trees. The Morrison Azalea Garden, at the intersection with Eagle Nest Road, features a study collection of large-flowered Japanese hybrids. After the intersection, Azalea Road becomes Crabtree Road.

2.1 Turn left onto Ellipse Road.

Here you'll find a majestic and picturesque "ruin" created from the Corinthian columns removed from the U.S. Capitol Building during renovation of the east front during the Kennedy administration. The 14-ton columns were designed by Benjamin Latrobe. Set on this hill and surrounded by understated gardens, they form the closest thing to the Acropolis this side of Athens.

Return to Crabtree Road.

2.9 Fern Valley is on your left.

It features a self-guided nature trail along a stream, over a bridge, and past witch hazel, ferns, oaks, wild ginger, bloodroot, trilliums, Dutchman's breeches, stunted American chestnuts, mountain laurel, and hemlocks. Lock your bike in the rack provided.

3.1 Beech Spring Pond is home to ducks and other waterfowl. Its banks are lined with weeping willows. Don't take the road that skirts the pond. Instead, bear right onto Hickey Hill Road. Then continue on Hickey Hill Road.

3.3 Take the overlook loop (right) to the Kingman Lake Overlook high above the Anacostia River.

3.5 Lock your bike in the rack here.

Take the path through the camellias and the Asian collections to the cinnabar Chinese teahouse, which overlooks a man-made waterfall cascading into the Anacostia River. There's a restroom and a drinking fountain near the bike rack.

3.5 Follow Hickey Hill Road as it curves to the left.

Columns from the east front of the Capitol building, removed during renovation in the Truman administration, now adorn a hill at the National Arboretum.

4.0 Park your bike in the rack adjacent to Dogwood Circle.

Stroll down the trail that winds through the woods here. Then walk across the road to the Gotelli Dwarf and Slow-Growing Conifer Collection, about 1,500 tiny trees in a landscaped setting.

4.0 Back on your bike, follow Meadow Road down the hill, past the crape myrtles (left), past Heart Pond, named for its shape (right), and over the bridge that spans Hickey Run.

4.7 Just past the intersection with Ellipse Road, stop to tour the National Bonsai Collection on your right.

A bicentennial gift from Japan, these tiny trees include some that are hundreds of years old. There are both evergreen and deciduous trees in the collection. The latter lose their leaves in the fall, just as big trees do. The National Herb Garden, on your left, is a fascinating collection of herbs used for medicinal and culinary purposes. In the same area is a collection of old roses.

5.0 Return to the parking lot.

Bicycle Repair Service

The Bike Shop at District Hardware, 2003 P Street NW (202-659-8686)

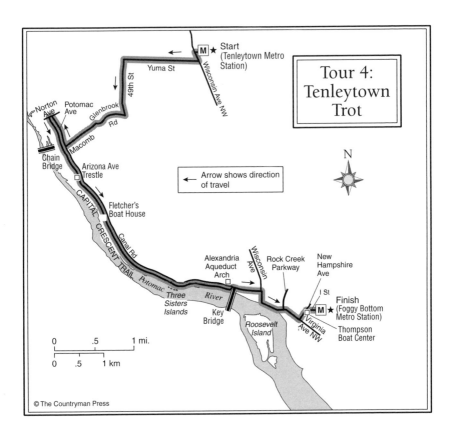

Start
(Tenleytown Metro Station)

Yuma St

49th St

Wisconsin Ave NW

Norton Ave

Potomac Ave

Glenbrook Rd

Macomb

Chain Bridge

Arizona Ave Trestle

Arrow shows direction of travel

CAPITAL CRESCENT TRAIL

Canal Rd

Fletcher's Boat House

Potomac River

Three Sisters Islands

Alexandria Aqueduct Arch

Wisconsin Ave

Rock Creek Parkway

New Hampshire Ave

I St

Finish
(Foggy Bottom Metro Station)

Key Bridge

Roosevelt Island

Virginia Ave NW

Thompson Boat Center

Tour 4:
Tenleytown
Trot

N

0   .5   1 mi.

0   .5   1 km

© The Countryman Press

4

Tenleytown Trot

LOCATION: Northwest Washington

METRO ACCESS: Start: Tenleytown; Finish: Foggy Bottom

TERRAIN: Mainly downhill and flat

ROAD CONDITIONS: A paved, off-road bike trail and (mainly) light-traffic streets

DISTANCE: 8.4 miles

HIGHLIGHTS: The pleasantly upscale Washington neighborhoods of Tenleytown, Spring Valley, Wesley Heights, and Palisades; spectacular views of the Potomac River, the Capital Crescent Trail, the Georgetown waterfront

By using Metro—or by planting cars at both ends of this trip—you can cheat Washington's geography and enjoy a mainly downhill ride. The tour starts at the Tenleytown Metro stop, situated in the shadow of the city's highest natural point, in Fort Reno Park. It then begins a downhill slope through the American University Park neighborhood that surrounds the institution of the same name, crosses into the posher quarters of Spring Valley, and then goes into the funkier but still upscale Palisades area. After a ride along the street on the edge of the palisades above the Potomac, the tour joins the Capital Crescent Trail and follows the river into Georgetown. The tour ends at the Foggy Bottom Metro station.

0.0 Exit the Tenleytown Metro station via the elevator and cross Albemarle Street NW and Wisconsin Avenue NW at the lights. Proceed south on Wisconsin Avenue.

0.1 Turn right onto Yuma Street, in front of St. Anne's Catholic Church.
The Oakcrest School will be on your right and an annex of American University on your left. Yuma Street is lined with neat, brick Colonial-style homes and goes steadily downhill.

1.0 At the bottom of the hill, turn left onto 49th Street.
Just before 49th Street crosses Massachusetts Avenue NW, look to your left at the small shopping center. Wagshall's Market there makes excellent sandwiches. After crossing Massachusetts Avenue, there's another opportunity for refreshment at Sutton Place Gourmet (left). You are now in Spring Valley, one of Washington's most upscale neighborhoods.

1.5 49th Street dead-ends. Turn right onto Glenbrook Road, a heavily treed street with large, sprawling houses set back from the road.
The road goes downhill, then up, crosses busy Loughboro Road, then heads downhill again.

Bear left onto Macomb Street and continue downhill into the Palisades neighborhood.

2.6 Cross busy MacArthur Boulevard.
This artery was originally called Conduit Road because of the aqueducts that ran underneath, carrying Washington's water supply. It was renamed for the World War II hero.

3.0 Macomb Street dead-ends at Potomac Avenue, at the edge of the palisades that tower over the river.
Relatively modest homes with million-dollar views sit on the east side of the street, leaving the river side open. From here, you can gaze down on a three-tiered view. Just below you is the Capital Crescent Trail, replete with in-line skaters, strollers, and cyclists. Below that, separated by woods, are the C&O Canal and towpath. And below that, the Potomac rolls over boulders and dams into Washington.

Turn right onto Potomac Avenue.

3.5 Potomac Avenue dead-ends at Norton Avenue, in front of the Dalecarlia Reservoir. Follow the well-worn dirt path next to the reservoir fence, which leads to the Capital Crescent Trail. Turn left onto this paved trail, the area's newest rails-to-trails product (see Tour 6).

The Capital Crescent Trail has brought new life to an abandoned rail spur that once carried freight between Georgetown and Silver Spring.

4.5 The trail crosses the Arizona Avenue Trestle, a 19th-century engineering wonder.

Look down at the C&O Canal and towpath. After traversing the trestle bridge, the trail runs side by side with the towpath, and many people cross from one to the other.

5.0 Fletcher's Boat House offers restrooms and refreshments.

On your left, accessible by crossing the canal on a footbridge, stands the Abner Cloud House, built in 1801. The Clouds lived upstairs and used the basement to store grain and flour from a nearby mill Abner Cloud operated. The trail continues, veering slightly downhill and getting close to the river.

6.5 In midriver, look for the Three Sisters Islands, favorite haunts of recreational boaters.

In the early 1970s, a plan to build a bridge at this point was defeated by conservationists. Look downriver for views of the Key Bridge, the Rosslyn skyline, and the Kennedy Center for the Performing Arts.

7.1 The Capital Crescent Trail ends near the ruins of the old Alexandria Aqueduct Arch in Georgetown.

Built in 1843, the bridge carried barges across the river to another canal that led to the port of Alexandria. In 1886, it was converted to an automobile bridge, and in 1933, it was replaced by the nearby Key Bridge.

Continue in the same direction on K Street, a former industrial area of Georgetown, under the elevated Whitehurst Freeway.

7.5 At Wisconsin Avenue (left), turn right toward the waterfront, then left along a gravel path that leads to the glitzy Washington Harbor development.

Walk your bike along the sometimes crowded walkway, past restaurants and shops. In midriver (right) lies Theodore Roosevelt Island, a wildlife sanctuary dedicated to the conservationist president.

Just before Thompson Boat Center, turn left into the parking lot for the same facility. Cross Rock Creek Parkway at the light and continue up Virginia Avenue.

You'll pass the notorious Watergate complex, venue of the break-in that eventually toppled Nixon and residence of intern fatale Monica Lewinsky.

8.1 Turn left onto New Hampshire Avenue. Turn right onto the I Street pedestrian mall.

Enter the Foggy Bottom Metro station via the elevator.

Bicycle Repair Service

Hudson Trail Outfitters, Ltd., 4530 Wisconsin Avenue NW (202-363-9810)

5

Brookland Bike-About

LOCATION: Northeast D.C.

METRO ACCESS: Brookland/CUA on the Red Line

TERRAIN: Moderately hilly

ROAD CONDITIONS: Light-traffic city streets

DISTANCE: 8.3 miles

HIGHLIGHTS: The Brooks Mansion, the National Shrine of the Immaculate Conception, the Pope John Paul II Cultural Center, Rock Creek Cemetery, turn-of-the-century homes, the Ralph Bunche House, the Franciscan Monastery

Brookland today is known as Washington's "Little Rome"—home of more than 60 Catholic institutions. But its history goes back even earlier than the 1880s, when the Catholic University of America was established here. In 1840, Colonel Jehiel Brooks, a veteran of the War of 1812, built a Greek Revival farmhouse on land purchased from the Caddo Indians. In 1870, the B&O Railroad ran its western branch line right by the Brooks Mansion, and developers followed in its wake, creating a rail-accessible "suburb in the city" and naming it after Brooks. Today, Metro brings commuters from downtown offices to homes in this diverse community, which has retained many of its original houses.

The tour begins at the Metro station (with an alternate start in the parking lot of the National Shrine), views the Brooks Mansion, which is not open for tours, visits the National Shrine and the Pope John Paul II Cultural Center, passes between the Old Soldiers' Home and adjacent National Cemetery, and enters Rock Creek Cemetery to view the Adams Memorial and other prominent graves. Then it loops back through

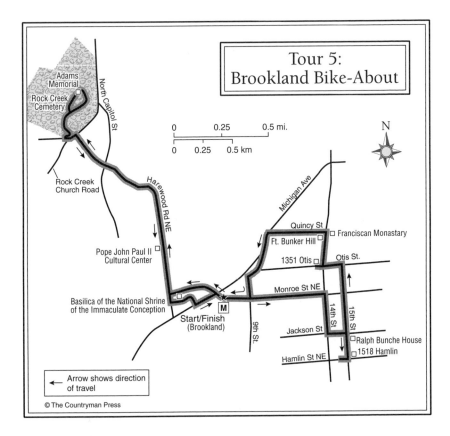

residential Brookland, sampling domestic architecture and stopping at the Franciscan Monastery before returning to the Metro station.

0.0 Exit the Metro Station using the exit marked BUSES.

The Brooks Mansion, currently leased to a public access television station, is on your right. Across Monroe Street NE stands Colonel Brook's Tavern, a latter-day watering hole and restaurant named after the builder of the mansion.

0.1 Turn left onto Monroe Street NE and follow it across the bridge over the Metro tracks to the intersection with Michigan Avenue NE.

0.3 Turn left onto Michigan Avenue.

0.4 Turn right into the Basilica of the National Shrine of the Immaculate Conception.

The mother church of Roman Catholicism in the United States, the shrine was dedicated in 1959 and is the largest Catholic church in the western hemisphere. The opulent 77,000-square-foot Byzantine-style structure features superb mosaics, including the centerpiece "Christ in Majesty," made up of nearly 3 million tiles. It is open for tours and has a cafeteria.

After your visit, ride past the front of the shrine to the exit, turning right onto Harewood Road NE.

0.9 On your right is the Hartke Theater, site of excellent student productions and of the Summer Opera.

1.0 Turn left into the Pope John Paul II Cultural Center.
There is a bike rack near the bus parking entrance. The state-of-the-art center offers changing exhibits and memorabilia about the late pope, including his skis, c. 1985.

After your visit, return to Harewood Road NE and turn left, continuing up a hill lined with various religious institutions.

1.4 Harewood Road turns left at the T. Follow it past Bishop Carroll High School and across North Capitol Street NE. It winds between the Old Soldiers' Home (left) and the National Cemetery, whose military graves line up straight as soldiers.

2.9 Harewood Road dead-ends at Rock Creek Church Road. Cross Rock Creek Church Road at the light and enter Rock Creek Cemetery. Maps are available at the gatehouse.
Opened in 1719 as a burying ground for parishioners of St. Paul's Episcopal Church, this is the city's oldest cemetery. It now serves the wider community. Among its denizens: Charles Corby, the inventor of Wonder Bread; Julius Garfinckel, founder of the downtown department store; Gilbert H. Grosvenor, president of the National Geographic Society; Supreme Court justices John Marshall Harlan, Harlan Fiske Stone, and Willis Van Devanter; Alice Roosevelt Longworth; Alexander "Boss" Shepherd, territorial governor of the District of Columbia; and Pulitzer Prize–winning author Upton Sinclair. Perhaps the best-known grave is the Adams Memorial, commissioned by writer Henry Adams for his wife, Marian, a suicide. The sculpture is by Augustus Saint-Gaudens. To reach the Adams Memorial, turn right after the gatehouse and take the road that goes to the church, the only surviving colonial church in Washington, dating from 1775. At the drive that goes up to the church, turn right at the sign indicating "Section E." Follow the

road as it rounds a corner, then take the first path up a small hill to the memorial, which is surrounded by yew trees. Though it's often called "Grief," the proper name of the sculpture is The Mystery of the Hereafter and The Peace of God that Passeth Understanding.

After your visit, exit the cemetery and re-enter Harewood Road NE, crossing North Capitol Street.

5.0 Turn right at the T, following Harewood Road down a hill.

5.6 At Ward Hall, turn left into the parking lot and onto the Catholic University campus, continuing past the rear of the National Shrine.

6.0 Turn right and exit the campus onto Michigan Avenue NE. Cross Michigan Avenue at the light and bear left on Monroe Street NE. Follow Monroe Street over a bridge and up a hill past grand old Queen Anne–style homes with gracious front porches.

6.5 Turn right on 14th Street NE, which goes down a hill.

6.6 Turn left on Jackson Street NE.
At 1510 Jackson Street stands the Ralph Bunche house, former residence of the Nobel Peace Prize winner and statesman and a good example of the International Style. Unlike most Brookland residences, it is of brick construction. The house was designed by noted African-American architect Hilyard Robinson, who studied in Europe with Walter Gropius, and was built in 1941, when Bunche was teaching at Howard University.

After viewing the house from the street, double back on Jackson Street and turn left on 15th Street NE.

6.9 Turn left on Hamlin Street NE.
At 1518 Hamlin Street stands a 1920 Sears, Roebuck and Co. catalog house, a good example of one of the many styles of Brookland domestic architecture.

After admiring the house from the street, double back on Hamlin and turn right on 15th Street, which climbs a hill.

7.4 Turn left on Otis Street NE.
At 1351 Otis Street is a Victorian cottage, another example of the neighborhood's architectural mix.

A cloistered arcade leads visitors into Washington's Franciscan monastary.

After viewing the cottage from the street, double back on Otis Street and turn left on 14th Street NE, which climbs a hill.

7.7 On the left is Fort Bunker Hill, now a park.

The fort was one of those that ringed Washington to defend the capital during the Civil War. It was built by the 11th Massachusetts Volunteer Infantry Regiment, which named it after the famous battle in the soldiers' home state. Thirteen guns and mortars were mounted here, but all evidence of them has disappeared.

7.8 On your right is the Franciscan Monastery, one of Washington's very special places.

Situated on 44 beautifully planted and landscaped acres, this Byzantine-style church, modeled on Istanbul's Hagia Sofia, was built in 1899. It is open daily, and tours start hourly. The church is surrounded by a cloistered arcade and gardens of roses and other flowers. In back of the shrine, in a leafy, parklike setting, are replicas of important Catholic shrines, such as the Grotto of Lourdes.

After touring the church or wandering around the grounds, go straight ahead at the exit and head down Quincy Street NE.

8.1 Turn left on Michigan Avenue NE.

8.2 Just before the bridge, turn left on 10th Street NE.

8.3 Turn right into the Brookland/CUA Metro station.

Bicycle Repair Service

Capitol Hill Bikes, 709 8th Street SE (202-544-4234)

City Bikes, 2501 Champlain Street NW (202-265-1564)

6

The Bicycle Beltway

LOCATION: Northwest D.C. and Montgomery County, Maryland

METRO ACCESS: Foggy Bottom

TERRAIN: Gentle uphill climb at the start, then flat or downhill

ROAD CONDITIONS: Paved off-road bike trails, a gravel off-road bike trail with a few "portages" on suburban streets

DISTANCE: 21.4 miles

HIGHLIGHTS: Georgetown waterfront, Potomac River, Fletcher's Boat House, the Arizona Avenue Trestle, the Dalecarlia Tunnel and Reservoir, Bethesda restaurants, Rock Creek Park, the Miller Cabin, Peirce Mill

To motorists, "the Beltway" connotes gridlock, heartburn, and road rage. But bicyclists now have a very different kind of beltway, a pastoral, tree-shaded, scenic inner loop that links Georgetown with Bethesda and then ambles back to town through bucolic Rock Creek Park. The 21-mile loop begins at the Foggy Bottom Metro station, accesses the Georgetown waterfront through the Thompson Boat Center, then enters the Capital Crescent Trail, a paved, multiuse pathway built along the abandoned Georgetown Branch, a railway spur completed in 1910 to link Georgetown with the main B&O line at Silver Spring. When the Capital Crescent Trail ends, the tour continues on an interim, gravel trail called the Georgetown Branch Trail, then connects with the Rock Creek Trail for a trip that follows that babbling brook back to the starting point.

0.0 Exit the Foggy Bottom Metro station, turning right. Cross 24th Street and turn left onto New Hampshire Avenue NW.

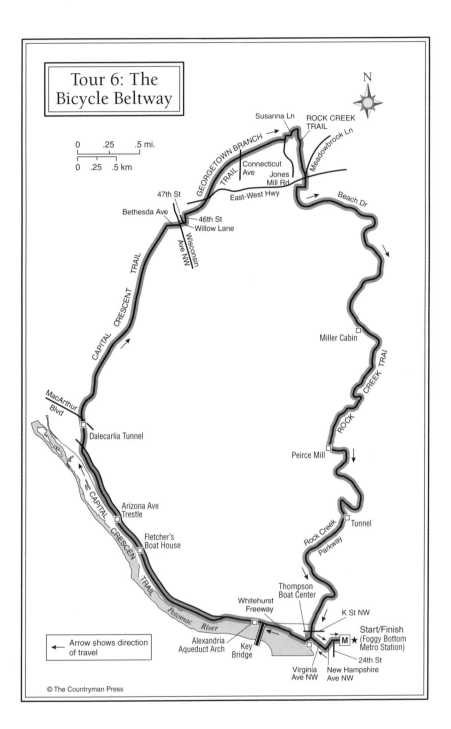

Tour 6: The
Bicycle Beltway

0   .25   .5 mi.

0   .25   .5 km

Susanna Ln   ROCK CREEK
              TRAIL

GEORGETOWN BRANCH

Connecticut
Ave

Jones
Mill Rd   Meadowbrook Ln

47th St   East-West Hwy   Beach Dr

Bethesda Ave

46th St
Willow Lane

Wisconsin
Ave NW

CAPITAL   CRESCENT   TRAIL

Miller Cabin

ROCK   CREEK   TRAIL

MacArthur
Blvd

Dalecarlia Tunnel

Peirce Mill

CAPITAL   CRESCENT   TRAIL

Arizona Ave
Trestle

Fletcher's
Boat House

Tunnel

Rock Creek
Parkway

Thompson
Boat Center

Whitehurst
Freeway

K St NW

Start/Finish
(Foggy Bottom
Metro Station)

Alexandria
Aqueduct Arch

Key
Bridge

M

24th St

Virginia
Ave NW

New Hampshire
Ave NW

Potomac   River

Arrow shows direction
of travel

© The Countryman Press

0.1 Turn right onto Virginia Avenue NW.

0.3 Cross Rock Creek Parkway at the light and enter Thompson Boat Center, where rental bikes are available. Go through the parking lot and turn left along the waterfront, walking your bike in front of the trendy restaurants.
The walkway will lead you to K Street NW, under the Whitehurst Freeway.

Turn left onto K Street.
Some parking is available here on Sundays.

0.7 After passing under the Key Bridge and the Alexandria Aqueduct Arch, the remains of an 1,100-foot aqueduct that once carried boats from the C&O Canal across the Potomac into Virginia, enter the Capital Crescent Trail.
The trail is paved and popular not only with cyclists but also with in-line skaters, dog walkers, and families with strollers. At the outset, it parallels the C&O Canal towpath, running between the canal and the river.

2.8 Fletcher's Boat House (left) offers refreshments and restrooms. Parking and bike rentals are also available here.

3.3 The Arizona Avenue Trestle carries the trail over the canal and Canal Road.
According to the trail brochure, the trestle spans are "outstanding examples of 19th-century pin-connected Whipple trapezoidal design." Past this point, the trail starts curving east, away from the river and toward Bethesda.

4.8 The Dalecarlia Tunnel, completed in 1910, carries the trail under MacArthur Boulevard.
Note the decorative brick facing at both ends. As you emerge, look to your right for a view of the Dalecarlia Reservoir, a key link in Washington's water supply. The trail continues beside Little Falls, a stream destined for the Potomac.

6.0 On your right is a marker for the site of Loughborough Mill.
One Nathan Loughborough came to the Federal City from Philadelphia in 1800, looking for work. He built a flour mill at this location in 1830, using the wheat that arrived in Georgetown on the canal barges. Loughborough Road is named for this family, which fled south during the Civil War.

7.8 After crossing River Road on a bridge and biking through the backyards of

Bethesda, the trail emerges at Bethesda Avenue in the heart of downtown Bethesda.

Restaurant choices abound here. The Thyme Square Cafe, at 4735 Bethesda Avenue, emphasizes vegetarian haute cuisine. To continue the tour, enter a tunnel that takes the trail under Wisconsin Avenue and enter the interim Georgetown Branch Trail, which is packed gravel.

The trail goes downhill through woods and meadows and along the perimeter of the Columbia Country Club.

9.2 The trail emerges at Connecticut Avenue. Cross Connecticut at the light and turn left.

9.3 Re-enter the trail between an Exxon station and a bank.

10.0 The trail emerges at Jones Mill Road. Turn left onto Jones Mill, then right onto Susanna Lane.

10.2 Turn right onto the Rock Creek Trail, which follows the stream into a park with athletic fields and playgrounds.

10.9 Cross East-West Highway and enter Meadowbrook Lane.

11.0 On your right are the Meadowbrook Stables.

Ride around the stables, bearing left alongside the playground. There are restrooms in the log house next to the playground.

11.1 Cross the footbridge in front of the log house and turn left onto Beach Drive.

12.2 Beach Drive crosses the District line.

In the District, Beach Drive is closed to cars on weekends. It winds through the park, beside the ever-widening creek. Picnic groves, available to groups by reservation, line the road.

15.0 On your right is the Miller Cabin.

Built by rough-hewn Joaquin Miller, "The Poet of the Sierras," the log cabin originally stood in Meridian Hill Park on 16th Street, but was moved here courtesy of the California State Society. Poetry readings are held here on occasion.

16.6 Enter the off-road trail to your right.

A cyclist enters the Capital Crescent Trail, built on a railway spur completed in 1910.

16.8 Peirce Mill, the sole survivor of 26 gristmills powered by Rock Creek, stands on your right.

Restrooms and drinking fountains are available here.

18.3 The trail comes to a tunnel. Detour to the right on a wooded trail through the zoo grounds.

18.8 Rejoin the main trail.

20.1 The slope on your right is part of Oak Hill Cemetery.

The cemetery is the final resting place of many of Washington's elite, from "Home, Sweet Home" author John Payne to Washington Post publisher Philip Graham. The white-columned memorial modeled after Rome's Temple of Vesta is the tomb of Marcia Burns Van Ness, who died in the devastating cholera epidemic of 1832. There is no access to the cemetery from the trail.

20.2 The trail passes under the Buffalo Bridge. Look up at the sandstone faces of an Indian on the arch. The face was reportedly modeled on the death mask of Sitting Bull.

21.1 At the Thompson Boat Center, cross Rock Creek Parkway with the light and continue up Virginia Avenue.

21.3 Turn left onto New Hampshire Avenue.

21.4 Cross 24th Street and enter the Foggy Bottom Metro station to your right.

Bicycle Repair Service

The Bicycle Place, Inc., 10219 Old Georgetown Road, Bethesda, Maryland (301-530-0100)

Griffin Cycle, Inc., 4949 Bethesda Avenue, Bethesda, Maryland (301-656-6188)

Six-Trail Mix

LOCATION: Northwest Washington and Montgomery County, Maryland

METRO ACCESS: Foggy Bottom

TERRAIN: Mainly flat, with a few short uphill climbs

ROAD CONDITIONS: A hard-packed dirt trail, paved off-road and on-road trails, light-traffic streets

DISTANCE: 33.4 miles

HIGHLIGHTS: The Chesapeake and Ohio Canal towpath with locks and lockhouses; the Old Angler's Inn; upscale Potomac, Maryland, with shops, restaurants, and country clubs; the Clara Barton National Historic Site; Glen Echo Park; the Capital Crescent Trail; the Georgetown waterfront

This tour, which starts at the Foggy Bottom Metro station, makes use of six—count 'em, six—area bicycle trails. After a very brief ride on the Rock Creek Trail, it follows the granddaddy of all multiuse trails, the C&O Canal towpath, through leafy Georgetown and past the Beltway. It stops for an al fresco lunch at the fashionable Old Angler's Inn and, after a short stint on the on-road MacArthur Boulevard bicycle trail, it follows the off-road Falls Road bicycle trail into the center of horsy Potomac and onto the River Road off-road bicycle trail. The tour then swoops down Persimmon Tree Road, lined with million-dollar homes and country clubs, into the funkier but still classy Carderock neighborhood and rejoins the MacArthur Boulevard Trail, which leads past the restored home of Clara Barton and Glen Echo Park, an art deco–era amusement park turned arts center. After crossing the

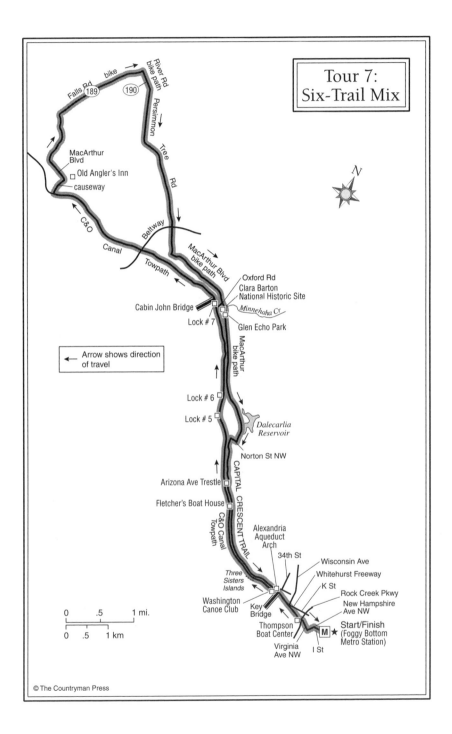

Tour 7:
Six-Trail Mix

bike
River Rd
bike path
Falls Rd 189 190
Persimmon
Tree Rd

MacArthur
Blvd
□ Old Angler's Inn
causeway

C&O
Canal
Towpath

Beltway

MacArthur Blvd
bike path

Oxford Rd
Clara Barton
National Historic Site

Cabin John Bridge
Lock # 7
Minnehaha Cr
Glen Echo Park

MacArthur
bike path

N

Arrow shows direction
of travel

Lock # 6
Lock # 5
*Dalecarlia
Reservoir*

Norton St NW

CAPITAL CRESCENT TRAIL

Arizona Ave Trestle
Fletcher's Boat House

C&O Canal
Towpath

Alexandria
Aqueduct
Arch

34th St
Wisconsin Ave
Whitehurst Freeway
K St
Rock Creek Pkwy
New Hampshire
Ave NW

*Three
Sisters
Islands*

Washington
Canoe Club
Key
Bridge

Thompson
Boat Center

Virginia
Ave NW
I St

M ★ Start/Finish
(Foggy Bottom
Metro Station)

0   .5   1 mi.
0   .5   1 km

© The Countryman Press

District line, the tour picks up the Capital Crescent Trail for a final descent back to the starting point.

0.0 Exit the Foggy Bottom Metro station via the elevator and turn right onto the I Street pedestrian mall. At the intersection, turn left onto New Hampshire Avenue, which still has some of the Victorian row houses of the old Foggy Bottom district.

This is what the whole neighborhood looked like before George Washington University and high-rise apartment houses encroached.

0.2 Turn right onto Virginia Avenue NW.

On your left is the Watergate complex, site of the infamous burglary that felled a president.

0.4 Cross Rock Creek Parkway in the pedestrian crossing and turn right on the Rock Creek bike path.

0.7 Across the parkway, on your right, stand the ruins of the Godey Lime Kilns, which processed lime brought to Georgetown on the Chesapeake and Ohio Canal from western quarries. Turn left into the C&O Canal towpath.

The Chesapeake and Ohio Canal, begun in 1828, stretches from the mouth of Rock Creek in Georgetown to Cumberland, Maryland, some 185 miles to the northwest. An elevated towpath, built 12 feet wide to accommodate the mule teams that pulled the canal barges, now accommodates hikers, joggers, horseback riders—and cyclists.

Follow the paved towpath through Georgetown.

You'll pass four lift locks, the embarkation point for the mule-powered boat that takes visitors on short canal rides, and some old brick houses now painted in rainbow colors and used as artists' studios and shops. One offers carryout food and ice cream cones.

1.6 At 34th Street, the towpath crosses the canal on a bridge and becomes a dirt trail.

Here the canal is lined with old warehouses and industrial buildings that have been turned into smart shops and condominiums.

1.7 After passing under Key Bridge, you'll see the Victorian-style clubhouse of the Washington Canoe Club on your left.

Busy Canal Road is on your right across the canal. Just beyond this point, Canal Road ceases to be a major thoroughfare, and the towpath becomes quieter, more countrylike.

3.8 On your left is Fletcher's Boat House.

It offers bike, canoe, and boat rentals and a snack bar. There are picnic tables and a pleas-ant lawn that leads down to a cove on the Potomac River.

4.5 Cross a wooden bridge over a canal spillway.

5.7 At Lock #5, the towpath crosses a bridge. Restrooms and a drinking foun-tain are available here.

6.1 The small, whitewashed house provided for the tender of Lock #6 is typical of these four-room residences, which were part of the compensation for the tenders.

A 1-acre garden plot came with the house. In addition, the canal company paid a salary that ranged from $100 a year to $75 a month. Boats signaled the tender with a bugle. In the canal's heyday in the 1870s, an average of more than a hundred boats a day passed through the locks. In 1835, the canal company's board ruled against hiring women to tend locks, feeling that the work was too strenuous. An exception was made for Elizabeth Burgess, who was hired to tend Lock #2 "providing that she hire a capable assistant."

In this area, the towpath stays close to the Potomac River, affording views of Little Falls Dam just upstream. Heed the posted warnings about staying out of the dangerous river.

7.1 On your left is the private Sycamore Island Club.

7.8 A wooden footbridge on your right is a good vantage point to watch turtles sunning themselves on the rocks below.

10.1 Just after passing Lock #7, the towpath goes under the Cabin John Bridge.

On your right after the bridge is the David Taylor Model Basin, used by the Navy to test the seaworthiness of ship designs. On your left is a large picnic area.

13.1 A wide causeway to your right leads to the Old Angler's Inn on MacArthur Boulevard.

During one of his celebrated hikes to save the canal from being paved over to create a highway, Justice William O. Douglas stopped here, with fellow canal aficionados, for lunch. Since the hikers were wet and dirty and not dressed in proper restaurant attire, the management turned them away. Now, however, the restaurant accommodates hikers and cyclists with tables placed outside, although the menu is pricey.

After lunch, continue heading west on the signed—but on-road—MacArthur Boulevard Trail.

The hills on this short stretch will work off anything you had for lunch.

14.1 Turn right onto Falls Road (MD 189), entering the bike path.

The path, largely shielded from the road by trees and other vegetation, leads through the tracts of million-dollar homes that make up Potomac, Maryland.

16.1 The bike path ends just before the intersection with River Road (MD 190).

There is a shopping center with carryout and restaurant food available.

Cross River Road and Falls Road in the pedestrian crossings and turn right onto River Road, entering the bicycle path that begins just past the gas station and the bank.

17.0 At the standing clock, turn right onto Persimmon Tree Road, which curves downhill past expensive homes and exclusive country clubs.

After crossing the Beltway on a bridge, you enter the funkier Carderock neighborhood and descend to MacArthur Boulevard.

20.9 Turn left onto the MacArthur Boulevard bike path.

22.0 Turn right onto Oxford Road to the Clara Barton National Historic Site.

The pleasant, yellow-clapboard house was built in 1891, of boards salvaged by the Red Cross from the great flood in Johnstown, Pennsylvania. It served as both home and office for American Red Cross founder Clara Barton, who got her start when, as a Patent Office clerk, she volunteered for duty in the field hospital set up in that office during the Civil War. After the war, she helped locate missing soldiers and lobbied for the adoption of the Geneva Convention. She retired to this house after a bitter bust-up with President Theodore Roosevelt over the Red Cross performance during the Spanish-American War, and died here in 1912.

After visiting the Barton house, continue across the parking lot to Glen Echo Park.

22.3 Cross Minnehaha Creek on a wooden footbridge, and follow the path into Glen Echo Park.

The first organized activity on this site began in 1891, with a Chautauqua Assembly "to promote liberal and practical education especially among the masses of the people" and, not incidentally, to sell lots and houses to the same masses. The park was promoted as the "Rhineland of the Potomac," but the bubble burst after rumors of malaria surfaced. Later, the site was transformed into an amusement park, with rides, a ballroom, and the Crystal Pool, which held three thousand people. The park closed in 1968, but most of the buildings still stand, and the National Park Service runs the historic Dentzel Carousel. Art groups now occupy most of the buildings.

22.6 Passing to the left of the stone tower, the only building remaining from the Chautauqua period, carry your bike up a set of stone steps and turn right onto the MacArthur Boulevard bike path.

23.4 Continue on the bike trail past the Army mapping facility and the Dalecarlia Reservoir and across the District line.

25.7 Just past the reservoir, turn right onto Norton Street NW.

25.8 Where Norton Street dead-ends, turn right onto a dirt path and walk your bike down to the Capital Crescent Trail.

25.9 Turn left onto the trail, which runs downhill toward the Potomac.

Through the woods to your right, you can catch glimpses of the C&O Canal and towpath and the river.

26.8 The trail crosses Canal Road and the canal on the Arizona Avenue trestle.
This double-span bridge is supposed to be a superb example of 19th-century pin-connected Whipple trapezoidal design.

30.0 Fletcher's Boat House is on your right.
Fletcher's Boat House rents bikes and boats, sells refreshments, and offers restrooms. Picnic tables and fishing spots are available along the Potomac. On your left stands the Abner Cloud House, the oldest along the canal. The trail and the towpath run side by side for a stretch. Watch for traffic crossing from one to the other.

31.5 On the river, to your right, look for three rocky islets, known as the Three Sisters.
Plans to build a bridge at this spot were thwarted in the 1970s by conservationists.

32.1 The trail ends at the ruins of the Alexandria Aqueduct Arch.

The Abner Cloud House overlooks both the C&O Canal towpath and the Capital Crescent Trail.

The aqueduct once carried barges from the canal across the river and onward, by another canal, to the port of Alexandria. The aqueduct bridge was torn down in 1933 and replaced by the adjacent Key Bridge, a vehicular bridge.

Continue on K Street, under the Whitehurst Freeway and along the Georgetown waterfront.

32.5 Across from Wisconsin Avenue, turn right onto a path that leads toward the waterfront.

Follow it into the Washington Harbor complex of restaurants and shops, where you will have to walk your bike.

32.8 Just before Thompson Boat Center, turn left and exit through the parking lot, crossing Rock Creek Parkway at the light and continuing on Virginia Avenue NW.

33.1 Turn left onto New Hampshire Avenue NW.

33.3 Turn right onto the I Street pedestrian mall.

33.4 Enter the Foggy Bottom Metro station via the elevator.

Bicycle Repair Service

The Bicycle Pro Shop, 3403 M Street NW (202-337-0311)

8

Cycling through Arlington's History

LOCATION: Arlington County, Virginia, with a few blocks in Alexandria and Falls Church

METRO ACCESS: Pentagon City; to do the tour in two segments, ride from Pentagon City to the East Falls Church Metro station the first day and complete the tour by riding from East Falls Church to Pentagon City the second day

TERRAIN: Mainly flat and rolling with a few hills

ROAD CONDITIONS: Paved bike paths and suburban streets

DISTANCE: 23.6 miles

HIGHLIGHTS: The Arlington Historical Museum, the view from Prospect Hill, Sparrow Swamp, Carlin Hall, the Ball-Sellers House, Carlin Springs, the Southern Railway caboose, the Bon Air Rose Garden, two District of Columbia boundary stones, Maple Shade, the Glebe, Dark Star Park, the Iwo Jima Memorial, Arlington National Cemetery

On the map, Virginia's Arlington County looks like the missing puzzle piece that completes the District of Columbia's diamond shape. Indeed, what we now know as Arlington was Virginia's contribution to the capital district, ceded in 1801. That's only one of the historical facts you'll learn on this ride adapted from the Arlington History Bicycle Ride with the kind permission of tour designer Randy Swart. In addition to two of the boundary stones that marked the old borders of the District of Columbia, the tour takes in Arlington's oldest residence—a log cabin built in 1742 with later additions; Maple Shade, a grand home damaged by Union cannons during the Hall's Hill skirmish in the

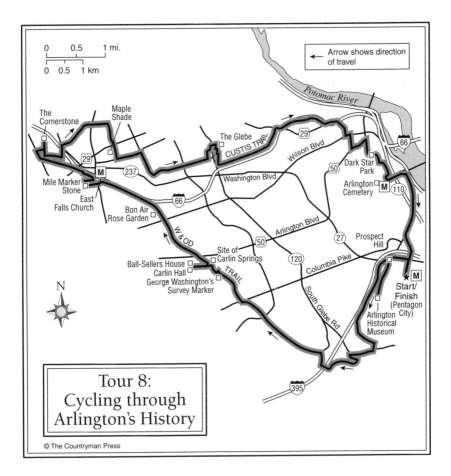

© The Countryman Press

Tour 8:
Cycling through
Arlington's History

Civil War; the Glebe, a farm provided to the rector of Fairfax Parish and later used as a hunting lodge; and many other local landmarks. It starts either at the Pentagon City Metro station or in the parking lot of the Arlington Historical Museum at 1805 South Arlington Ridge Road. For more details of Arlington history than can fit on these pages, go to www.bscl.org/histride.htm.

0.0 Exit the Pentagon City Metro station and turn right onto South Hayes Street, which has an on-street bike lane.

0.1 Turn left onto Army-Navy Drive.

0.2 At Joyce Street, cross to the left side of the road and continue on the sidewalk, following Army-Navy Drive up a hill.

0.5 Turn left on South Lynn Street and left again on Arlington Ridge Road.

1.0 Turn left into the parking lot of the Arlington Historical Museum.
The museum is housed in the old Hume School, built in 1891 in the Queen Anne style, and is open on weekends. It contains three floors of exhibits on local history and is staffed by knowledgeable volunteer docents. After your visit, exit the parking lot and turn right on Arlington Ridge Road.

1.2 On your right, at the intersection of Arlington Ridge Road and South Lynn Street, stand the castlelike remnants of the Little Tea House, where old-time Arlingtonians used to go for refreshments and to enjoy the view. The view is now obstructed by high rises, and the remnants have been incorporated into an apartment house pool complex. Continue to the end of Arlington Ridge Road to enjoy the view from Prospect Hill, where a quarry owner built a grand home that was destroyed during the Civil War. From this vantage point, you can see many of the monuments in Washington as well as the Pentagon and busy Shirley Highway.

1.3 Turn left onto South Nash Street and left again at the intersection with Army-Navy Drive for a long downhill coast.

2.5 Turn left onto South 28th Street, which runs beside a park and through a residential neighborhood.

3.0 Turn right onto South Meade Street.

3.1 Cross South Glebe Road at the light and turn right onto the Four Mile Run Trail.

3.5 Cross West Glebe Road and turn left, riding on the sidewalk.

3.8 Turn right onto Valley Drive, which becomes Martha Custis Drive.

4.3 Carry your bike up the stairs and take the pedestrian bridge across Shirley Highway, I-395.

4.5 On the other side of the bridge is the Village of Shirlington shopping center, with many restaurants. Turn right onto South Quincy Street and follow it to the intersection with Arlington Mill Drive. Cross the road and turn left onto the Four Mile Run Trail.

5.3 At Walter Reed Drive, turn right and continue one block.

5.4 Cross Four Mile Run Drive and turn left onto the Washington and Old Dominion (W&OD) Trail, a rail trail.
The trail leads through meadows and woods and very gently climbs up the fall line that divides Tidewater Virginia from the Piedmont. Beside the trail, a stream courses down the fall line.

7.0 Benches at the Sparrow Pond viewing deck offer a seat for observing water lilies and turtles.

7.1 Exit the trail on a path to the left, which leads to the Long Branch Nature Center. Continue through the parking and picnic areas.

7.3 Bear right and continue up a steep hill. At the top of the hill, jog right and then turn left onto 4th Street South and continue three blocks.
Just past South Kensington Street stands Carlin Hall, a frame "Stick Style" house built in 1892 as a community center for the Arlington neighborhood of Glencarlyn, developed in the late 1800s by George Curtis and Samuel Burdette.

7.6 Turn around and go back on 4th past the library and turn left onto South Kensington Street and right onto 3rd Street South to the John Ball House, sometimes called the Ball-Sellers House, at 5620 3rd Street South.
This is Arlington's oldest residence, built c. 1742 by John Ball, one of the area's original colonial settlers, who received a grant of 166 acres from Lord Fairfax. William Carlin,

George Washington's tailor, bought the house from Ball in 1772. The part of the house to the left as you face it is the original log cabin, later covered with siding. A cutout in the wall shows the original logs. The two-story portion on the right was added c. 1885. The house is owned by the Arlington Historical Society and is open Saturday afternoons from April to October. Call 703-379-2123 for the latest information on opening times.

7.8 Continue down South 3rd Street and turn left on South Jefferson Street, riding down a hill. At the bottom of the hill, turn onto a paved path to your right, which leads through woods into Four Mile Run Park.

7.0 At the bottom of the hill, walk your bike across a wooden bridge to the original site of Carlin Springs, where the Carlin family developed an amusement park—complete with swimming hole, dance floor, restaurant, and ice cream parlor—in 1872. The park was served by a branch of the Washington & Old Dominion railroad, which brought families here for Sunday outings. After viewing the site, backtrack to the path and re-enter the W&OD Trail, turning left.

8.9 At the old Bluemont Junction, where passengers from another line originating in Rosslyn disembarked to board the Washington & Old Dominion line, stands a big red Southern Railway caboose. On weekend afternoons, a volunteer train buff spins rail lore and gives tours of the caboose.

9.0 Continue on the trail under Wilson Boulevard, then loop up to the left to the sidewalk and cross Four Mile Run. Turn left on North Lexington to the Bon Air Rose Garden, which has more than three thousand rose plants and is gloriously abloom in June. After your visit, double back and continue on the trail, which runs along I-66, in a series of small, roller coaster–type hills.

10.4 After making sharp left and right turns in Madison Manor Park, pass under Sycamore Street and, ignoring the W&OD Trail's turn to the right, continue straight to the end of the trail stub onto North Van Buren Street.

11.0 Turn right on North Van Buren and stop at Benjamin Banneker Park.
The park features a small boundary stone enclosed by a 2-foot iron fence. The stone was placed here in 1791 to mark the southwest corner of the nation's new capital, the District of Columbia. The park is named for the African-American man who assisted Andrew Ellicott in laying out the capital city. After exiting the park, continue on North Van Buren and turn right on 18th Street North.

11.4 Turn left onto North Tuckahoe Street and right onto the W&OD Trail, which passes the East Falls Church Metro station and crosses Lee Highway at a light.

12.0 Exit the trail and turn right on Great Falls Street.

12.1 Turn right on North Dorchester Road and left on North Meridian Street.

At the end of the block, in Andrew Ellicott Park (left), stands the District's west boundary stone, again enclosed by a iron fence. The original 10-square-mile District of Columbia was formed by land contributed by both Maryland and Virginia. In 1847, the land on the west side of the Potomac River was given back to Virginia. Originally, the area returned to Virginia was called Alexandria County, but in 1920 it was renamed Arlington County. After admiring the stone, turn back along Meridian Street to North Lincoln Avenue and turn left. North Lincoln becomes Fairfax Drive and re-enters Arlington from Falls Church.

12.9 Turn left on Westmoreland Street, which crosses under I-66, and turn right onto 28th Street North.

13.0 At the top of a small hill, bear left on Little Falls Street, which passes Bishop O'Connell High School and goes around a traffic circle. After crossing Sycamore Street, Little Falls becomes 28th Street North again.

13.9 Turn right on North Powhatan Street, which crosses Lee Highway and goes down a hill.

14.4 At 2230 North Powhatan, stop to admire Maple Shade (right).

The now privately owned residence was built in 1851 by Captain Henry W. Febrey and damaged by a Union cannon during a skirmish. Continue down Powhatan to the end and enter a gravel path that leads to 22nd Street North. Turn left on 22nd Street North.

14.9 Turn right on North Lexington Street and follow it until it bears left at the top of a small hill and becomes 16th Street North. Follow 16th Street down a long hill and cross George Mason Drive.

16.4 Turn left onto North Abingdon Street, then right onto 17th Street North.

16.6 Cross North Glebe Road carefully and continue up a small hill to 4727 17th Street N, the Glebe (left).

In the Church of England, a glebe was a farm provided to a parish rector as part of his salary. This glebe, originally 500 acres, was given to the rector of Fairfax Parish and a

The Marine Corps War Memorial honors the heroes who raised the flag on Iwo Jima.

house was built here in 1775. The house burned down in 1808 and, in 1820, was replaced by a hunting lodge. The octagon wing was added c. 1850. The white teak eagle peering from the roof was placed there by diplomat Caleb Cushing, who received it as a gift while serving as ambassador to Spain.

After your visit, turn right on North Wakefield Street, across 17th Street from the Glebe.

16.7 Follow North Wakefield Street as it jogs left.

17.0 Turn left onto the Custis Trail, which parallels I-66 and goes up and down several hills and around curves.

19.4 Exit the trail and turn right onto Scott Street, which crosses I-66 on a bridge and becomes Key Boulevard.

19.6 Turn right on Quinn Street and take the first left onto 18th Street North.

19.7 Take the trail to the right, which leads through Rosslyn Highlands Park to Wilson Boulevard. Cross Wilson Boulevard and continue down North Pierce Street.

20.0 At the bottom of the hill, turn left on Fairfax Drive, a service road for Arlington Boulevard.

20.2 At the corner of Fort Myer Drive stands Dark Star Park, which contains sculptures by Nancy Holt. The large stone spheres represent stars that have fallen from the sky, "dark stars." Turn right and take Fort Myer Drive over the bridge, where it becomes Meade Street.

20.6 Cross Meade Street and enter the trail that leads to the Marine Corps War Memorial, popularly known as the Iwo Jima Monument.

The statue sets in bronze a photograph taken by Associated Press combat photographer Joe Rosenthal, a native Washingtonian. The Pulitzer Prize–winning picture shows six Marines raising the American flag atop Mount Suribachi, the highest point on the small island of Iwo Jima and the scene of bloody fighting in 1945. Three of those Marines survived the battle and later posed for sculptor Felix de Weldon. De Weldon sculpted likenesses of the three dead Marines from photographs.

Adjacent to the memorial is the Netherlands Carillon, a gift from the people of the Netherlands in recognition of U.S. aid during World War II.

After viewing the carillon, follow the bike trail that leads along the wall of Arlington National Cemetery.

21.2 The trail emerges at the road that leads to Arlington National Cemetery and its visitor center, which has restrooms and drinking fountains.

If you want to tour the cemetery and Arlington House, lock your bike at the rack along the road leading to the parking lot. You can take a commercial shuttle bus tour of the cemetery or walk up the hill to visit Arlington House, the Kennedy graves, and the Tomb of the Unknowns. Before entering Arlington House, walk to the edge of the bluff to the grave of Major Pierre L'Enfant, architect of the Federal City. Another Frenchman, the Marquis de Lafayette, described the vista from here as the "finest view in the world." Built between 1802 and 1817 by George Washington Parke Custis, a descendant of Martha Washington, the house was named for the ancestral Custis estate on the eastern shore of Virginia. It passed to his daughter, Mary Anna Randolph Custis, who married a young West Point graduate named Robert E. Lee. It was here at Arlington House, in his bed-room on the second floor, on the night of April 19, 1861, that Lee made his painful and fateful decision to resign from the U.S. Army and join the Confederate forces. Two days later, he left for Richmond, never to return to Arlington House. The estate was confis-cated in 1864, and a military cemetery was started on the grounds. After the war, a de-scendant of the Lees sued the government for return of the property—and won. But since the military graves surrounding the house made it unattractive as a dwelling, he accepted a settlement of $150,000.

Of special interest in the mansion is the White Parlor. The decor of this room shows the influence of the time Lee spent in Mexico during the Mexican-American War.

After your visit, return to your bike and turn right, out of the road to the parking lot, onto Memorial Drive. At the traffic circle, ride on the sidewalk, crossing two highways in crosswalks.

21.7 Turn right on the bike path.

21.8 When you come to the sign directing the bike path to the left, ignore it and bear right, following the path over a series of bridges.

22.1 With the Pentagon looming ahead, continue on the path, which crosses the road twice, in crosswalks, and leads along a fence around the Pentagon. When the path ends at a barrier, jog left and continue straight, through a Pentagon parking lot.

22.9 At the end of the parking lot, turn left.

23.0 Turn right and walk your bike through a pedestrian tunnel into a parking lot for the Pentagon City shopping complex. Turn right and ride around the perimeter of the lot, exiting onto Army-Navy Drive.

23.1 Turn left on Army-Navy Drive and right on South Hayes Street.

23.6 At the corner of 12th Street South, cross Hayes Street and enter the elevator for the Pentagon City Metro station.

Bicycle Repair Service

Metropolis Bike and Scooter, the Village at Shirlington, Arlington, Virginia (703-671-1700)

9

Along the Potomac to Mount Vernon

LOCATION: Northern Virginia

METRO ACCESS: Ronald Reagan National Airport

TERRAIN: Mostly flat with a few hills approaching Mount Vernon

ROAD CONDITIONS: A paved, off-the-road bike path except for a short stretch on city streets through Alexandria, where there will be light-to-moderate traffic on weekends

DISTANCE: 28.8 miles

HIGHLIGHTS: Potomac River views, Old Town Alexandria, Dyke Marsh, River Farm, Mount Vernon

If George Washington had owned a bicycle, this trail to Mount Vernon might have been completed a lot sooner than it was—in 1973. If you ignore the cars zipping by on the George Washington Memorial Parkway and focus your attention on the river side of the trail, you'll find that the views aren't radically different from those the first president would have seen. The 17-mile trail actually starts at Theodore Roosevelt Island. This tour begins a few miles downriver at the Ronald Reagan National Airport Metro stop.

0.0 Exit the Metro station and follow signs to the bike trail.

Although the trip begins in an airport-industrial milieu, the trail soon breaks out into a plethora of pleasant river views. Approaching Daingerfield Island, you seem to sail into the proverbial "forest of masts."

1.3 Turn left to the Washington Sailing Marina on Daingerfield Island, which is no longer a real island.

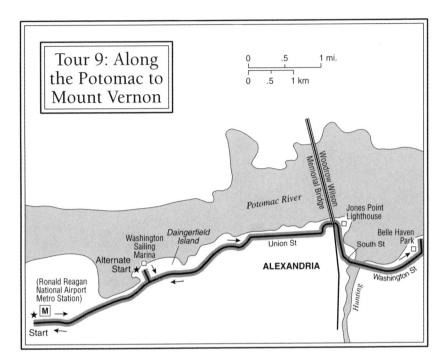

Tour 9: Along the Potomac to Mount Vernon

This 107-acre park holds an excellent restaurant, Potowmack Landing, which also has an informal snack bar plus picnic tables, restrooms, water fountains, phones, and playing fields. There is also a large parking lot, which makes this a good place to begin for people who prefer car starting points to Metro starting points.

2.1 The trail breaks temporarily in Old Town Alexandria, but signs guide you along city streets. After passing Oronoco Bay Park, a waterfront area with picnic tables, turn left onto Pendleton Street and take an immediate right onto North Union Street.

3.0 On your left stands the Torpedo Factory, a World War II munitions operation that now houses craft shops, studios, and galleries.

Hitch your bike to a street sign and browse, stroll along the waterfront, and walk up King Street (right) for window shopping and information and walking-tour maps at Ramsay House Visitors Center, 221 King Street. Housed in the home of William Ramsay, a Scottish merchant and city founder, the visitor center can provide information on and directions to other Old Town attractions, including two homes of Robert E. Lee; Christ Church, attended by both Washington and Lee; Gadsby's Tavern, where Washington

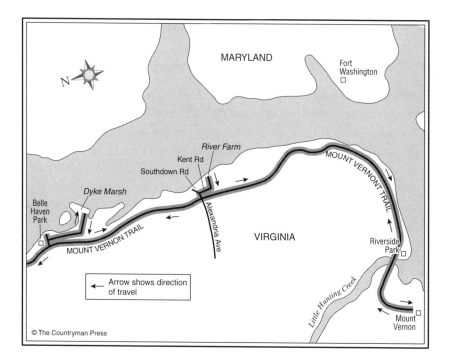

used to sip Madeira; and the Stabler-Leadbeater Apothecary Shop Museum, where Martha Washington used to buy medicines.

4.0 At Gibbon and Union Streets, the off-the-road bike trail resumes, leading you through the woods, back along the river, and past an old Ford plant that is now a spiffy residential development.

4.3 Keeping left, along the river and under the Woodrow Wilson Memorial Bridge, you'll see the Jones Point Lighthouse, which warned sailors of nearby sandbars from 1836 to 1925.

Look along the seawall for the cornerstone that once marked the southernmost corner of the District of Columbia.

Turn right and follow the road directly under the Wilson Bridge to South Street. Turn left.

4.8 Turn left onto Washington Street, following the marked trail.

You'll pass some large apartment complexes, cross Hunting Creek, and be treated to a sweeping vista of the wide Potomac.

5.5 The trail leads through Belle Haven Park, site of an 18th-century settlement of Scottish tobacco merchants.

Wide green lawns, a marina, picnic tables, and restrooms are available.

Turn left onto the road that leads to Belle Haven Marina, and then make an immediate right onto a dirt trail that leads through Dyke Marsh.

Dyke Marsh is a wetland sanctuary and the last large tidal freshwater marsh in the Washington area. Except after very heavy rains, the trail is passable for touring bikes. The first encroachment on the marsh's natural state came in the early 1800s, when a settler tried to turn the wetland into farmland by building earthen dikes around it. These were soon abandoned as too costly, and the land reverted to its natural—wet—state. Ride quietly and you may catch glimpses of frogs, turtles, beavers, muskrats, rabbits, shrews, field mice, foxes, and more than two hundred species of birds.

6.2 The Dyke Marsh Trail ends at the river. Reverse direction and return to the main bike trail.

6.9 Turn left onto the marina road and left again onto the Mount Vernon Trail.

7.3 The trail enters a boardwalk that skirts Dyke Marsh.

9.1 The trail exits the woods and enters a small residential enclave.

Trail signs direct cyclists across a bridge on Alexandria Avenue, but a short detour will allow a visit to River Farm.

Instead of crossing the bridge, continue straight on Southdown Road.

9.2 Bear right onto Kent Road.

9.7 Turn left into River Farm, the headquarters of the American Horticultural Society.

The house dates from 1757 but was much altered in the 1920s. George Washington bought the property in 1760, gave it its name, and later presented it to his personal secretary, Tobias Lear, as a wedding gift. The house is open for special exhibits. The grounds and beautiful gardens are open summer weekends, and the public is welcome to picnic by the river, under trees that Washington may have planted.

9.9 After your visit, reverse direction and return to the intersection of Southdown Road and Alexandria Avenue.

10.7 Turn left and cross the Alexandria Avenue bridge. Once across, turn left again, following the trail signs.

The trail stays close to the parkway, skirting some quiet residential neighborhoods, then enters a wooded area and climbs a hill.

12.9 Rest on a bench and drink in the view of Fort Washington, an early 19th-century bastion on the Maryland shore.

You'll go up and down a few curvy hills, then cross to the river side of the parkway again.

14.7 Riverside Park, at the point where Little Hunting Creek empties into the widest point of the river you've glimpsed so far, offers picnic tables as well as views.

Rest up for some uphill climbs and downhill coasts.

15.8 Proceed with caution through the large Mount Vernon parking lot to the mansion entrance, probably with a stop at the restrooms and snack bar first.

The mansion is open daily including Christmas, and there is an admission fee. In addition to the mansion itself, which contains the bed in which George Washington died, attractions include boxwood gardens, the smokehouse, and the slave burial ground.

Unless you have arranged for someone to pick you up, you'll have to double back along the trail.

27.5 Arrive at Washington Sailing Marina.

28.8 Arrive at Ronald Reagan National Airport Metro station.

Bicycle Repair Service

Big Wheel Bikes, 2 Prince Street, Alexandria, Virginia (703-739-2300)

Bikes USA, 1506-C Belle View Boulevard, Alexandria, Virginia (703-768-3444)

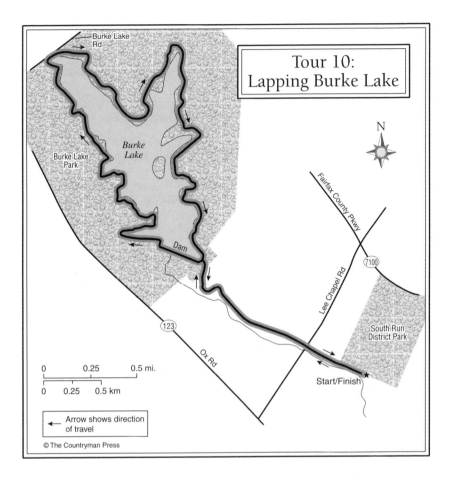

Tour 10:
Lapping Burke Lake

N

Burke Lake
Rd

Burke
Lake

Burke Lake
Park

Dam

Fairfax County Pkwy

Lee Chapel Rd

7100

South Run
District Park

123

Ox Rd

Start/Finish

| 0 | 0.25 | 0.5 mi. |
| 0 | 0.25 | 0.5 km |

Arrow shows direction
of travel

© The Countryman Press

10

Lapping Burke Lake

LOCATION: Fairfax County, Virginia

TERRAIN: Rolling hills with one steep climb

ROAD CONDITIONS: Hard-pack-dirt and paved trails

DISTANCE: 7.1 miles; many cyclists go around the lake trail, a distance of 4.5 miles, more than once

HIGHLIGHTS: Bucolic Burke Lake with its many coves and indentations and its resident and migratory waterfowl

Hidden among the upscale subdivisions of Fairfax County is this jewel of a park with a 214-acre lake that looks like something out of the north woods. A hard-packed dirt trail meanders 4.5 miles around the lake, winding into every nook and cranny and providing great views of the water and of Vesper Island, a waterfowl refuge. It's a great family ride and a great ride for getting in shape at the beginning of the cycling season. To add a little mileage, this tour actually starts at South Run District Park, which is linked to Burke Lake Park by a paved trail. To get to the starting point, take Beltway exit 54A, Braddock Road West. Turn left on Burke Lake Road and left again on Lee Chapel Road. Make another left onto Fairfax County Parkway and follow to the park entrance on the right. The trail begins behind the recreation center.

0.0 Enter the paved trail, which leads downhill, through woods and along a fast-running stream. Ignore the unmarked side trails, which lead into neighborhoods, and follow the main trail straight ahead and up a slight hill.

1.3 Turn left on the hard-packed dirt trail along the dam at the end of Burke Lake, looking right to admire the pristine lake and shoreline.

1.9 The trail crosses a park road and goes up a slight hill, past volleyball courts and a playground.

2.2 The trail crosses another park road and continues along the lake shore, hugging coves and inlets. It winds close to the lake, and benches and viewing areas are placed at intervals.

3.4 At the end of the lake, bear right, crossing a feeder stream on a bridge and continuing on the trail on the other side, which runs along the lake next to a camping area.

4.0 The trail veers sharply to the left, along a fingerlike inlet, and then to the right, through a wilderness camping area.

5.0 A bench just off the trail provides a good view of Vesper Island, a waterfowl sanctuary.

5.8 At the dam, bear right on the paved trail, following it down a winding hill and along the stream.

7.1 After climbing a steep but short hill, the tour returns to South Run District Park.

Bicycle Repair Service

The Bike Lane, 9544 Old Keene Mill Road, Burke, Virginia (703-440-8801)

Burke Lake Park offers lakeside benches.

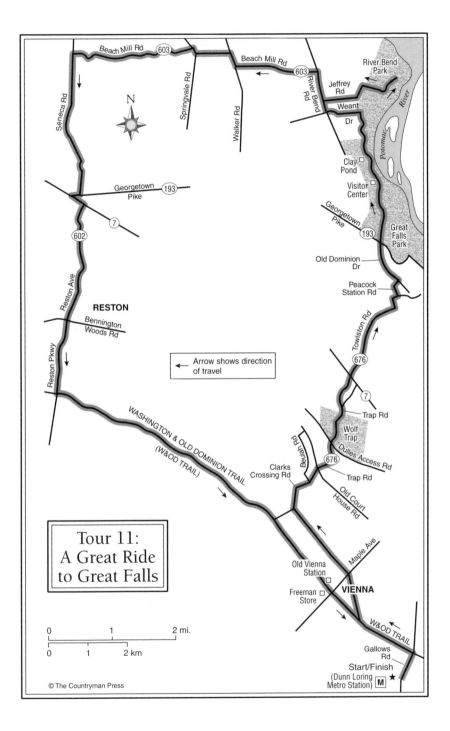

Tour 11:
A Great Ride
to Great Falls

© The Countryman Press

11

A Great Ride to Great Falls

LOCATION: Northern Virginia

METRO ACCESS: Dunn Loring

TERRAIN: Hilly

ROAD CONDITIONS: Paved trail and roads with mainly light traffic

DISTANCE: 36 miles

HIGHLIGHTS: The Great Falls of the Potomac, Riverbend Park, Reston, Vienna, the Washington and Old Dominion Trail

On its way to the sea from the mountains of West Virginia, the Potomac River really picks up speed as it approaches Washington—dropping 80 feet in less than a mile and roaring through Mather Gorge in a rush of churning whitewater. This point on the river, known as Great Falls, has long attracted visitors, who come to gaze at the raw power of nature, to picnic, fish, hike, rock climb, or even boat in the whitewater below the falls. At the turn of the century, the Washington and Old Dominion Railroad built a branch line to carry excursionists to the falls, where an inn, a dance pavilion, and a carousel added to the natural attractions. Today the railroad, the inn, the pavilion, and the carousel are gone, but the park is still so popular that the parking lot is sometimes full—and closed to visitors—by noon.

You can avoid Great Falls gridlock by cycling to the falls, on a route that takes advantage of the Washington and Old Dominion Trail—the roadbed of the main line of the railroad to Great Falls—and travels for a short distance on Old Dominion Drive, the roadbed of the spur to Great Falls. After a visit to Riverbend Park, a quieter spot on the Potomac upstream from the falls, the tour continues through the hills of northern Virginia, runs through the pioneer planned community of

Reston, and rejoins the W&OD Trail for a visit to Vienna, a town that has honored its railroad past by restoring a caboose, which stands adjacent to the trail.

Appropriately enough, this tour begins at a Metrorail stop, the Dunn Loring station, which affords easy access to the W&OD Trail.

0.0 Exit the Dunn Loring station, turning left onto Gallows Road. There is a paved trail along the road.

0.7 Turn left onto the W&OD Trail.
Although it traverses a suburban area, the trail is pleasantly wooded. Watch for wild Turk's-cap lilies, which burst into blossom in July.

2.0 A historical marker indicates the spot where the railroad was first used to carry troops into battle during the Civil War. Union troops were riding on flatbed cars in the early days of the war, scouting for enemy troops. A South Carolina regiment heard the train approaching, and a brief skirmish ensued. Casualties were minor, but Union troops had to walk back to Washington because the frightened engineer put the train into full reverse and left without them.

3.1 The trail crosses Maple Avenue.
Restaurants and food stores are available on this street, the main thoroughfare of Vienna.

Cross Maple at the stoplight and continue on the trail.

4.9 Exit the trail to the right through the small parking lot that lies across the trail from the Clarks Crossing soccer field and park. Proceed along Clarks Crossing Road.

5.7 Clarks Crossing Road stops at Beulah Road. Turn left onto Beulah Road.

5.8 At the stop sign, Beulah Road turns left. Cross Old Court House Road and continue straight on Trap Road (VA 676).

6.4 At the stop sign, follow Trap Road to the left.
You'll pass the Barns at Wolf Trap, part of the Filene Center for the Performing Arts, which is administered by the National Park Service.

6.2 After crossing over the Dulles Access Road on a bridge, Trap Road passes the main part of Wolf Trap Farm Park.

The location of a popular outdoor summer theater, the park was once the farm of Mrs. Jouett Shouse, who donated it to the nation.

7.7 Trap Road turns right. Follow Towlston Road, which continues straight ahead as VA 676.

8.2 Towlston Road crosses VA 7 and winds through an area of large homes set back from the road.

8.6 Turn left onto Peacock Station Road.

8.9 Peacock Station Road ends. Turn left onto Old Dominion Drive, following the route the railroad to Great Falls used to take.

10.6 Old Dominion Drive crosses Georgetown Pike and continues down a hill and through the woods into Great Falls Park.

11.5 Stop at the tollbooth to pay a small admission fee and to pick up a trail map before proceeding straight ahead to the visitor center.

The visitor center has exhibits on the geology and history of the area, plus restrooms, a snack bar, and a bookstore. Lock your bike at the rack outside the visitor center and walk to the overlook for a spectacular view of the falls. Look downstream for kayakers daring the white water. Near the observation platforms are ruins of some of the workings of the Patowmack Canal, a pet project of George Washington. Construction on this Great Falls bypass began in 1786 and was completed two years after Washington died—giving reality to his frequent toast: "Success to the navigation of the Potomac!" Unfortunately, the high cost of building his canal eventually bankrupted the company, and the route was abandoned in 1830, leaving the way open for the Chesapeake and Ohio Canal on the Maryland side of the river (see Tour 7).

After leaving the visitor center, continue to the end of the parking lot. On your left, you will see Clay Pond.

11.7 Turn left onto the paved fire road at the head of Clay Pond.

The road soon turns to easily negotiable dirt and gravel and winds uphill through the woods.

12.7 The trail ends at Weant Drive. Turn left and be prepared for a series of roller-coaster hills.

13.3 Turn right onto River Bend Road (VA 603).

13.5 Turn right onto Jeffery Road, which makes a left and then turns right into River Bend Park.

14.3 Proceed past the tollgate (no fee for bikes) to the visitor center.

The visitor center has a snack bar and picnic tables on a deck that overlooks a sweeping lawn leading down to the Potomac.

After seeing the fury of Great Falls, you may find it hard to believe that this is the same river only a mile or so upstream. It's quite tranquil here, with boats for rent and a nature center.

After a respite in this pretty and peaceful park, double back on Jeffery Road, riding through the park gates to the intersection with River Bend Road.

16.3 Turn right onto River Bend Road.

16.8 River Bend Road ends. Turn left onto Beach Mill Road, the continuation of VA 603.

18.3 Beach Mill Road seems to end, but really doesn't. Turn right onto Walker Road.

18.4 Turn left and pick up Beach Mill Road again. This is an area of large homes and horse farms.

19.0 Continue across Springvale Road on Beach Mill Road, which enters a very hilly phase, winding past expensive-looking, brand-new "chateaux."

21.2 Beach Mill Road ends. Turn left onto Seneca Road (VA 602).

Look to your right for spectacular views of distant blue mountains.

23.3 Seneca Road ends at Georgetown Pike (VA 193). Follow Georgetown Pike to the right for about a hundred feet, then cross VA 7 at the light. Turn left onto VA 7, riding on the shoulder to the frontage road.

23.5 Turn right onto Reston Avenue, the continuation of VA 602.

There is a food store at the intersection. When it enters the thriving "new town" of Reston, Reston Avenue becomes Reston Parkway. Laid out in 1892 by Dr. Carl Adolph Max Wiehle, who acquired a 7,200-acre tract here with a partner, the town did not become a reality until the early 1960s.

With a mighty roar, the Potomac River careens down the fall line at Great Falls, Virginia.

25.3 At the intersection with Bennington Woods Road, a paved bike path begins, running parallel to Reston Parkway.

It continues, with a few interruptions, to the intersection of Reston Parkway and the W&OD Trail.

26.5 Turn left onto the W&OD Trail, which runs through fields and over lowlands crisscrossed by small streams.

Listen for frogs and watch for river otters and herons. A stone-arch bridge carries the trail over Piney Branch.

32.7 On your left is the old Vienna railroad station, which is currently leased to the Northern Virginia Model Railroaders Association.

These hobbyists are in the process of modeling a section of the Western North Carolina Railroad, complete with operating trains, scenery, and buildings. Several times a year, the railroaders hold an open house at the old station to show visitors their work-in-progress (call 703-938-5157 for dates and information). On the other side of the trail stands a bright red refurbished caboose, which the town of Vienna acquired after Virginia repealed the law requiring manned cabooses on trains.

32.8 On your right, at the corner of Church Street and the trail, stands the Freeman Store.

This emporium dates to 1859 and is now operated as a general store by Historic Vienna, Inc. It's open Sundays from noon to 5 PM and sells crafts, handmade items, and penny candy. The house also served as the town's post office and as its first railroad station. During the Civil War, the building was occupied by both Northern and Southern troops as the village, with its strategically important railroad, changed hands frequently.

32.9 The trail crosses Maple Avenue, Vienna's main artery.

The town, settled in the 1760s by Scots and originally called Ayr Hill, was rechristened Vienna in 1858 by a doctor who had lived in Vienna, New York, and studied medicine in Vienna, Austria. Although part of the mushrooming Washington suburban area, Vienna retains its small-town charm.

35.3 Turn right onto Gallows Road.

36.0 Turn right into the Dunn Loring Metro station.

Bicycle Repair Service

Nova Cycle, 124 Maple Avenue West, Vienna, Virginia (703-938-7191)

12

A Virginia Triangle

LOCATION: Arlington and Alexandria, Virginia

METRO ACCESS: Arlington Cemetery

TERRAIN: Gradual uphill climbs at the start, then downhill or flat

ROAD CONDITIONS: Paved off-road bike trails with a few "portages" on suburban streets

DISTANCE: 16.2 miles

HIGHLIGHTS: Bluemont Park, Four Mile Run, the Ronald Reagan National Airport terminal, views of the Washington Monument, Lincoln Memorial, Kennedy Center

The great thing about the proliferation of bike trails in the Washington area is that you can mix and match them, creating tours that require only short stints on city and suburban streets. This triangle-shaped tour uses parts of four bike trails: the I-66/Custis Trail, the Bluemont Junction Trail, the Four Mile Run Trail, and the Mount Vernon Trail. After a gradual climb at the outset, the tour glides downhill, following Four Mile Run as it changes from a tree-shaded babbling brook to a broad tidal creek. The last few miles follow the Potomac River upstream, with spectacular views of Washington at every turn.

The tour begins in the parking lot for Theodore Roosevelt Island, accessible from the northbound lanes of the George Washington Parkway. The nearest Metro stop is Arlington Cemetery. Or, from the District, you can ride your bike across Memorial Bridge and take the Mount Vernon Trail north to Roosevelt Island.

0.0 Exit the Roosevelt Island parking lot and follow the I-66/Custis Trail up a ramp and through busy Rosslyn.

The paved trail winds uphill through commercial strips and residential neighborhoods.

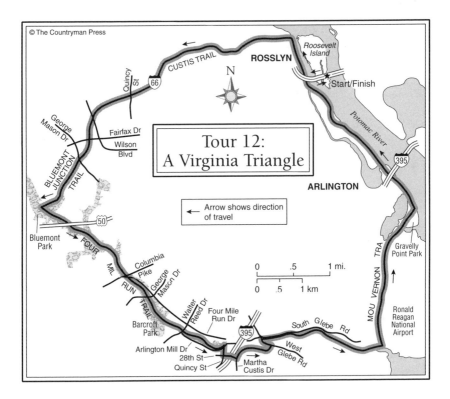

3.5 At the crest of a hill, turn left, following the sign for the Bluemont Junction Trail.

If you come to George Mason Drive, you have missed the turnoff, so go back. This spur will take you downhill to the sidewalk along busy Fairfax Drive in the Ballston section of Arlington. Ballston is a good place to find food.

3.6 Cross Fairfax Drive in the crosswalk that leads to the Holiday Inn. Turn right, doubling back on the opposite side of the street. Then take the first left onto the Bluemont Junction Trail, which goes through a small park.

3.7 Where the park ends, cross both George Mason Drive and Wilson Boulevard and pick up the trail to your right.

Continue through wooded and meadowlike parkland bordered by the backyards of diverse Arlington, sharing the trail with families pushing strollers and shepherding kids on training wheels.

4.6 The trail crosses Four Mile Run Drive and runs into a large athletic field. *This is the junction with the Four Mile Run Trail.*

Turn left and continue through beautiful Bluemont Park.

4.9 Here you will find clean, modern restrooms.
The trail follows the stream through woods and alongside gardens. Watch for garter snakes on the trail.

6.2 The trail crosses Columbia Pike.
A few yards to your left before crossing the Pike is the Town Express Carryout, with Asian, Spanish, and American food. Try the Vietnamese summer rolls.

6.7 Turn right onto George Mason Drive and cross the bridge that goes over Four Mile Run.

6.8 Turn left onto the trail through Barcroft Park, a lovely wooded area with picnic tables.

7.7 Emerge from Barcroft Park and continue on the trail to your left. Cross Walter Reed Drive at the light.

8.4 At the trail sign, cross Arlington Mill Drive on your left and continue one block on Quincy Street through the booming Shirlington area, which offers many restaurants. Turn left onto 28th Street, and then make an immediate left onto the overpass that will take you to the other side of I-395.

8.8 At the other side of the overpass, turn left onto Martha Custis Drive, a low-traffic residential street through a suburban neighborhood.

9.3 Martha Custis Drive dead-ends on West Glebe Road. Go left onto the sidewalk along West Glebe Road.

9.5 At the busy intersection of West Glebe Road, Four Mile Run Drive, and South Glebe Road, cross West Glebe Road to the right and follow the trail, which runs between Four Mile Run—the stream—and South Glebe Road.

The Mount Vernon Trail hugs the Potomac shoreline, affording great views across the river of Washington.

You will traverse small parks and ride along the backs of garden apartments. Watch Four Mile Run grow broader and become a habitat for waterfowl, a sure sign that the Potomac is coming up.

11.6 After passing a water treatment plant with educational signs explaining its operation and going under several low bridges, look to your right to see Four Mile Run flow into the Potomac River. Round a curve and join the Mount Vernon Trail at Ronald Reagan National Airport. Head north in the direction of Washington, D.C. Follow the trail through Gravelly Point Park, a popular picnic spot, and continue along the Potomac.

Across the river, you'll see the Washington, Jefferson, and Lincoln Memorials and the Kennedy Center.

16.2 Return to the Roosevelt Island parking lot.

Bicycle Repair Service

Metropolis Bicycles, 4056 South 28th Street, Arlington, Virginia (703-671-1700)

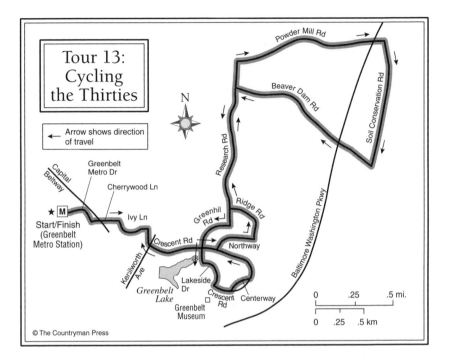

Tour 13:
Cycling
the Thirties

← Arrow shows direction
of travel

N

Powder Mill Rd →

Beaver Dam Rd

Soil Conservation Rd

Research Rd

Capital Beltway

Greenbelt Metro Dr

Cherrywood Ln

M

Ivy Ln →

Start/Finish
(Greenbelt
Metro Station)

Kenilworth Ave

Crescent Rd →

Greenhil Rd

Ridge Rd

Northway

Baltimore Washington Pkwy

Greenbelt
Lake

Lakeside
Dr

Crescent
Rd

Centerway

Greenbelt
Museum

0   .25   .5 mi.

0   .25   .5 km

© The Countryman Press

13

Cycling the Thirties

LOCATION: Prince George's County, Maryland

METRO ACCESS: Greenbelt

TERRAIN: Moderately hilly in the Beltsville Agriculture Research Center; almost flat in Greenbelt

ROAD CONDITIONS: On-road bicycle trail and light-traffic roads

DISTANCE: 14.4 miles

HIGHLIGHTS: Country roads in the Beltsville Agricultural Research Center; the planned New Deal town of Greenbelt, with its art moderne architecture

One day in the '30s, brain-truster Rexford G. Tugwell took President Franklin Delano Roosevelt for a ride in the country around Washington. He showed him a site adjacent to the Agricultural Research Center at Beltsville and proposed that a "garden community" be built there for low- and middle-income families, so that they could live in a "green belt" convenient to but apart from cities. Greenbelt, Maryland, was one of three such places built in the United States, and it is still a thriving community, though no longer under federal control.

This tour starts at the Greenbelt Metro station, follows a well-marked bike trail to the town, and visits both the adjacent Agricultural Research Center and historic Greenbelt, with a stop at the museum.

0.0 From the Metro station, proceed through the parking lot toward the exit on Cherrywood Lane.

0.4 Turn left onto Cherrywood Lane.

0.6 Cross Cherrywood Lane in the crosswalk. Turn left and cross the bridge over the Capital Beltway.

0.9 Turn right onto Ivy Lane, which has a marked bike lane and leads through an industrial park.

1.2 Where the bike lane ends, turn right, following Greenbelt's Cross City bicycle route signs.

1.4 Cross Kenilworth Avenue at the light and continue on Crescent Road, which has a path alongside the road.

2.3 At St. Hugh's Church, turn left onto Northway.

2.7 Turn left onto Ridge Road.

3.2 Turn right onto Research Road, ignoring the GATE CLOSED sign, which does not apply to cyclists.

The road leads to the U.S. Agricultural Research Center, more than 7,000 acres of woods and farmland used for researching methods to improve agriculture. The plump-breasted Beltsville turkey was developed here. The buildings and grounds are off-limits to the public, but the roads are open. Some of them are closed to automobile traffic on weekends, making for very pleasant cycling in a rural environment.

3.4 If the gate is closed, slide your bike under it and continue down a long hill.

4.3 Slide your bike under another gate and cross Beaver Dam Road. Continue on Research Road, which is lined with fields on one side, woods on the other.

4.6 Turn right onto Powder Mill Road, which carries automobile traffic but has a marked bike lane.

4.7 At the top of a hill, on your right, is a log lodge built by the Civilian Conservation Corps in 1936–1937.

The lodge serves as a visitor center, but is open only on weekdays.

6.0 Powder Mill Road crosses under the Baltimore Washington Parkway.

6.3 Turn right onto Soil Conservation Road.

6.7 Stop to admire the pigs lounging in the sun on your left.

7.5 Turn right onto Beaver Dam Road, which winds downhill through oak and pine woods.

9.3 Turn left onto Research Road, sliding your bike under the gate.

9.6 Stop and look to your left at the beaver dam. Then climb the hill you descended before.

10.2 Exit the Agricultural Research Center and continue on Research Road, crossing Ridge Road.

10.6 Turn right onto Greenhill Road, which curves downhill.

11.0 Cross Crescent Road and continue on a gravel path that leads to Greenbelt Lake. Cross over the end of the lake on a footbridge and continue up a path between houses.

11.2 Turn left onto Lakeside Drive.

11.5 Turn left onto Crescent.

11.7 Stop at 10-B Crescent Road (right) for the Greenbelt Museum, open Sunday 1–5 PM or by arrangement (301-474-1936).

The museum (admission free but donations accepted) is actually one of the original homes, built in 1937. At that time, the two-story house rented for $31 a month. Competition for the homes was stiff, and renters faced stringent rules. Wives had to agree to stay at home, and no laundry could be hung out on Sundays. The museum is furnished with the original 1930s appliances and "moderne" furniture from Scandinavia, which residents were encouraged to purchase in the local cooperative. Many of the museum docents are longtime residents of Greenbelt and give very informative tours.

On your left stands the old Greenbelt Elementary School, now the community center. The relief sculptures on the front of the building illustrate the Preamble to the Constitution. They were commissioned by the WPA and executed by sculptor Lenore Thomas.

Turn left into Centerway, entering the '30s-style shopping center with its co-op, credit union, and art moderne movie theater.

The centerpiece of the small mall is another Lenore Thomas sculpture entitled Mother and Child.

11.9 Exit the shopping center and turn left, continuing on Crescent Road.

13.1 Cross Kenilworth Avenue at the light and follow the bicycle path.

13.3 Turn left onto Ivy Lane.

13.6 Turn left onto Cherrywood Lane, taking the bike lane across the bridge.

14.4 Enter the Greenbelt Metro station parking lot.

Bicycle Repair Service

College Park Bicycles, 4360 Knox Road, College Park, Maryland (301-864-2211)

Heading off on the Headwaters Trails

LOCATION: Prince George's and Montgomery Counties, Maryland

METRO ACCESS: Alternative start at West Hyattsville

TERRAIN: Flat with one steep hill

ROAD CONDITIONS: Paved trails and suburban streets with shoulders, sidewalks, and light traffic on weekends.

DISTANCE: 18.5 miles

HIGHLIGHTS: Bladensburg Waterfront Park, wooded trails along the headwater streams feeding the Anacostia River, the Adelphi Mill and miller's cottage, the University of Maryland's flagship College Park campus, the 94th Aero Squadron Restaurant, historic College Park Airport and Aviation Museum

A 26-mile network of paved trails through mainly wooded parkland follows the headwater streams that feed the Anacostia River. Eventually, this network will be linked with trails along the river itself (see Tour 2). This tour travels on two of the headwaters trails: the Northeast Branch Trail and the Northwest Branch Trail. It begins at Bladensburg Waterfront Park, which marks the "head of tide" of the Anacostia River and is the place where four-masted schooners from Europe berthed until the river silted up in the mid-1800s (there is an alternative Metro start at West Hyattsville, mile 2.9). Crossing the Anacostia River on a pedestrian bridge, the tour heads up the Northeast Branch Trail, then veers west on the Northwest Branch Trail and follows it to its end. The tour then takes suburban streets and crosses the University of Maryland campus and rejoins the Northeast Branch Trail at College Park Airport. Bladensburg Waterfront Park is located

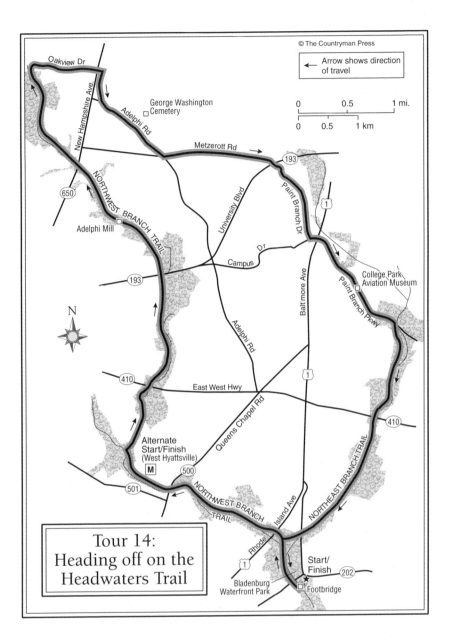

© The Countryman Press

Arrow shows direction
of travel

0   0.5   1 mi.

0   0.5   1 km

Oakview Dr

New Hampshire Ave.

Adelphi Rd

George Washington
Cemetery

Metzerott Rd

193

650

NORTHWEST BRANCH TRAIL

Adelphi Mill

University Blvd

Paint Branch Dr

1

Campus   Dr

193

N

Baltimore Ave

College Park
Aviation Museum

Paint Branch Pkwy

Adelphi Rd

410

East West Hwy

1

410

Queens Chapel Rd

Alternate
Start/Finish
(West Hyattsville)

M

500

501

NORTHWEST BRANCH
TRAIL

Island Ave

NORTHEAST BRANCH TRAIL

Rhode

1

Bladenburg
Waterfront Park

Start/
Finish

Footbridge

202

Tour 14:
Heading off on the
Headwaters Trail

at 4601 Annapolis Road (MD 450) in Bladensburg, near the Peace Cross.

0.0 From the parking lot in Bladensburg Waterfront Park, pick up the trail by the gazebo and head for the pedestrian bridge.

0.2 Once across the bridge, turn right onto the trail, which passes under a highway and through fields beside the Northeast Branch.

1.0 At the fork, follow the sign for the Northwest Branch Trail, proceeding left, up a rise and beside Armentrout Road.

1.3 Cross Rhode Island Avenue and proceed through Melrose Park.

1.9 The trail crosses 38th Avenue and enters 38th Avenue Neighborhood Park, proceeding through a meadowlike expanse.

2.2 The trail turns right onto a pedestrian bridge.

2.6 The trail turns right over another pedestrian bridge and then crosses Queens Chapel Road.

2.9 The trail passes the West Hyattsville Metro Station.

3.2 At the fork, bear right and cross a pedestrian bridge.

3.4 The trail to the left is the Sligo Creek Trail (see *25 Bicycle Tours in Maryland*). This tour goes straight on the Northwest Branch Trail.

5.3 Cross University Boulevard at the light.

6.0 After passing under Riggs Road, the trail emerges at the Adelphi Mill. *This grist mill was built in 1796 and later operated by George Washington Riggs, for whom the road is named. It is the oldest and largest mill in the Washington area. There is a picturesque miller's cottage next door. The mill is in a park and provides a good place for picnicking.*

8.2 At the end of the paved trail, turn right up a steep gravel hill.

8.8 The gravel trail ends in a suburban neighborhood. Continue on Oakview Drive.

9.5 Cross New Hampshire Avenue at the light.

9.6 At the top of a small hill, turn right on Mt. Pisgah Road and follow it downhill through a quiet neighborhood.

9.8 Bear left on Adelphi Road, riding on the sidewalk, and continue past Mt. Lebanon Cemetery.

10.4 At the intersection with Riggs Road, there's a shopping center with fast-food restaurants, a supermarket, and a convenience store. Continue on Adelphi Road, riding on the shoulder.

10.7 Turn left onto Metzerott Road, riding on the shoulder.

12.0 Cross University Boulevard at the light and enter Paint Branch Drive, which leads through the University of Maryland's College Park campus.

12.9 Turn left on Campus Drive and exit the campus and cross US 1, continuing straight ahead on Paint Branch Parkway.

14.0 On your right is the College Park Metro Station.

14.1 On your left is the College Park Aviation Museum, an affiliate of the Smithsonian Institution. Adjacent to it is College Park Airport.
The museum includes great old photographs and other artifacts of the world's oldest continually operated airport, opened in 1909 when the Wright brothers brought their plane here to teach Army officers to fly. In 1912, military pilot "Hap" Arnold made the first mile-high flight from here.

14.4 At left is the 94th Aero Squadron Restaurant.
The restaurant masquerades as a French farmhouse converted to a U.S. Army air post during World War I. An old ambulance graces the courtyard, and the decor is heavy on war-bond posters and similar memorabilia. Restrooms are called latrines. The view takes in the airport runways and is a good place to have lunch while you watch the Cessnas take off.

14.6 A left turn from the restaurant parking lot leads onto the Northeast Branch Trail. Head right on the trail, which follows the branch and passes under a bridge and into Riverdale Park.

16.0 Cross Riverdale Road.
The trail continues on a berm above the flood plain.

A cyclist crosses the Anacostia River at Bladensburg Waterfront Park.

17.0 Cross Decatur Street.

17.5 At the V go straight ahead on the Northeast Branch Trail.

18.3 Turn left onto the pedestrian bridge.

18.5 Exit the trail and return to the parking lot in Bladensburg Waterfront Park.

Bicycle Repair Service

Riverdale Cycle and Fitness, 4503 Queensbury Road, Riverdale, Maryland
(301-864-4731)

15

The One and Olney

LOCATION: Montgomery County, Maryland

METRO ACCESS: Forest Glen

TERRAIN: Hilly on roads, almost flat on bike trails

ROAD CONDITIONS: Some busy streets, most with sidewalks, bike lanes, or shoulders; three off-road trails, short stretches of dirt and gravel paths

DISTANCE: 33.2 miles

HIGHLIGHTS: Sligo Creek Trail, Brookside Gardens, the Olney Ale House, Rock Creek Park, Forest Glen Annex

This tour uses two of metropolitan Washington's vertical green-belts—Sligo Creek Park and Rock Creek Park—to escort you away from suburban sprawl and into a countrylike setting. Although getting there is half the fun, the destination is also very attractive: the cozy, funky Olney Ale House, host to travelers since 1924. The tour begins and ends at the Forest Glen Metro station of the Red Line, just outside the Beltway on Georgia Avenue.

0.0 Exit the Forest Glen Metro station and turn left onto Forest Glen Road, crossing busy Georgia Avenue at the light.

0.7 Turn left onto the Sligo Creek Trail. This multiuse paved trail runs on both sides of shady, sylvan Sligo Creek.

2.3 Cross University Avenue and continue on the trail, to your right.

3.0 The trail bears left, but this tour goes straight, on Orebaugh Avenue, following signs to the Wheaton Regional Park athletic complex.

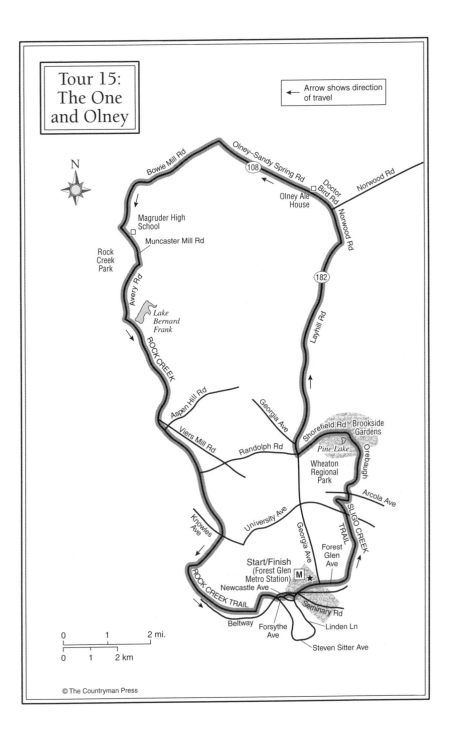

Tour 15:
The One
and Olney

Arrow shows direction
of travel

N

Bowie Mill Rd

Olney-Sandy Spring Rd

108

Doctor
Bird Rd

Norwood Rd

Olney Ale
House

Magruder High
School

Muncaster Mill Rd

Norwood Rd

Rock
Creek
Park

Avery Rd

182

Layhill Rd

Lake
Bernard
Frank

ROCK CREEK

Aspen Hill Rd

Georgia Ave

Shorefield Rd

Brookside
Gardens

Viers Mill Rd

Randolph Rd

Pine Lake

Orebaugh

Wheaton
Regional
Park

Arcola Ave

Knowles
Ave

University Ave

Georgia Ave

SLIGO CREEK TRAIL

Start/Finish
(Forest Glen
Metro Station)

M ★

Forest
Glen
Ave

ROCK CREEK TRAIL

Newcastle Ave

Beltway

Forsythe
Ave

Seminary Rd

Linden Ln

Steven Sitter Ave

0   1   2 mi.

0   1   2 km

© The Countryman Press

3.2 Cross Arcola Avenue and continue straight, following the road into Wheaton Regional Park, past tennis courts and a skating rink. Bear left after the skating rink onto a dirt-and-gravel road that leads past pretty Pine Lake.

Just past Pine Lake, to your right, lies Brookside Gardens. No bikes are allowed in the gardens, but you can lock your bike to the fence and walk through. The 50-acre facility includes a tropical conservatory, a Japanese garden with teahouse, an azalea walk, a rose garden, and an aquatic garden.

After your visit, continue on the paved trail, bearing right, up a hill.

4.3 Restrooms are available near the playground. Continue straight past the restrooms to the park exit.

4.5 Turn right onto Shorefield Road.

4.8 Turn right onto busy Georgia Avenue, riding on the sidewalk.

5.2 At a busy intersection, bear right onto Layhill Road (MD 182).

This moderately hilly road has a bike lane. It winds through a suburban area and gradually becomes more rural.

10.2 At the light in front of a liquor store (cold sodas available), turn left, with MD 182, onto Norwood Road.

11.1 Norwood Road turns right, but continue straight on MD 182, which becomes Doctor Bird Road.

12.0 At the intersection of Doctor Bird Road and Olney–Sandy Spring Road (MD 108) stands the Olney Ale House (right), a good destination for rest and refreshments.

This establishment was founded as the Corner Cupboard in 1924 and has offered food and drink to travelers ever since. It also serves patrons of the Olney Theater, a repertory and summer theater, across the road. It's so popular with cyclists that there's a bike rack. Seating is available either inside the pleasant sprawling house or outdoors.

After your stop, turn left in front of the inn and cross Doctor Bird Road at the light. Then head north on the off-road 108 trail, which runs alongside MD 108.

14.3 Turn left on Bowie Mill Road, which winds up and down hills.

17.6 At the light, turn left onto Muncaster Mill Road, which passes Magruder High School.

18.6 Turn right onto Avery Road, following signs to Rock Creek Regional Park. Ignore the two entrances to the park and stay on Avery Road.

20.2 Just past the entrance to Lake Bernard Frank, at the bottom of a wooded hill, turn left onto the Rock Creek Trail.

Follow this paved and shaded trail through the park. The trail clings close to the creek as it gurgles its way from the Montgomery County hills over rocks and boulders to its mouth on the Potomac in Washington. There are lots of green glades and nature-made beaches if you want to rest or wade.

22.9 Go through the parking lot and follow Aspen Hill Road to the intersection with Viers Mill Road. Cross Viers Mill Road at the light and continue on the trail.

24.8 Cross Randolph Road and continue on the trail.

26.7 At the intersection with Knowles Avenue, you can turn left and take an optional side trip to the Howard Avenue antiques district of Kensington.

This will add 1.4 miles to the trip.

30.7 Almost directly in front of you looms the Mormon Temple.

The exuberant, soaring white-marble structure is topped by a gilded trumpeting angel, Moroni. Mormons believe that Moroni lived in America in the fourth century AD and compiled the Book of Mormon. It was Moroni who appeared to Joseph Smith in 1827 and instructed him to found the Church of Jesus Christ of Latter-Day Saints. The temple was completed in 1974.

31.3 Just after passing under the Beltway, cross Jones Mill Road, ignoring the FOREST GLEN METRO sign. Turn left on Forsythe Avenue and left again on Newcastle Avenue.

At Linden Lane, turn right for a tour of the Forest Glen Annex of Walter Reed Army Medical Center.

The annex, once a resort, in 1924 became a girls' finishing school, the National Park Seminary. On the right side of Linden Lane stands a shingled frame pagoda, formerly a sorority house.

The Olney Ale House welcomes cyclists and other travelers.

After your tour, reverse direction and follow Linden Lane down the hill, out of the annex and across the Beltway.

32.3 After crossing both the railroad tracks and Seminary Road, turn right onto Forest Glen Road.

33.2 Turn left into Forest Glen Metro station.

Bicycle Repair Service

Griffin Cycle, Inc., 18050 Georgia Avenue, Olney, Maryland (301-774-3970)

16

Triadelphia Trek

LOCATION: Montgomery and Howard Counties in Maryland

METRO ACCESS: Shady Grove

TERRAIN: Moderately hilly to hilly

ROAD CONDITIONS: Mostly light traffic, some short rides on roads with heavy traffic; paved roads and some optional dirt roads

DISTANCE: 44 miles

HIGHLIGHTS: Historic Brookeville, Catoctin Vineyards, Triadelphia Reservoir, Brighton Dam

Brighton Dam blocks the Patuxent River to create Triadelphia Reservoir, a major source of water for 1.3 million people in Montgomery and Prince George's Counties. The Triadelphia watershed area also provides superb recreation and scenery. It's a mecca for fishermen and affords good picnic spots and places for people who want to get away from the hustle and bustle of the metropolis. There are no bike trails, and there is no road that hugs the shoreline, but it's possible to ride across the dam and around the reservoir on low-traffic roads with side trips for rests, picnics, and views of the water.

The trip starts at the Shady Grove station, about as far into the country as Metro will take you. In a short time after exiting the Metro station, you'll be in the country—although you'll never be far from encroaching development. Country roads will lead you through wooded areas, past small farms and babbling brooks to lovely, leafy Brookeville, a 19th-century town where people sit on wide front porches and watch the passing parade.

After a stop at Catoctin Vineyards, the closest winery to Washington, you'll be at the reservoir's edge. Please remember that swimming and

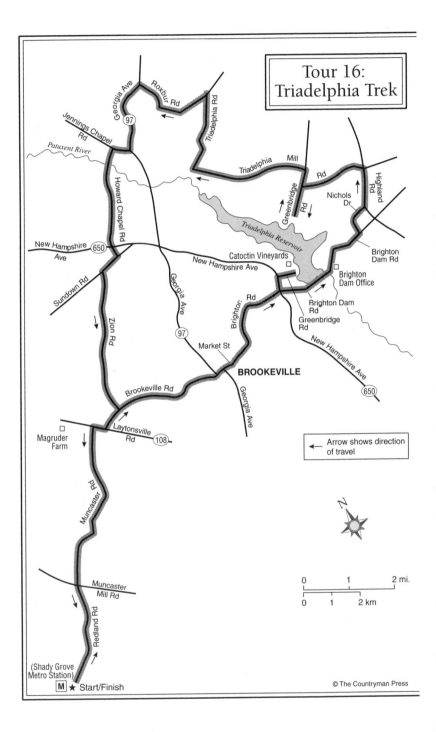

**Tour 16:
Triadelphia Trek**

Georgia Ave

Roxbur Rd

97

Triadelphia Rd

Jennings Chapel Rd

Patuxent River

Triadelphia Mill Rd

Howard Chapel Rd

Greenbridge Rd

Highland Rd

Nichols Dr

Triadelphia Reservoir

New Hampshire Ave

650

Catoctin Vineyards

New Hampshire Ave

Brighton Dam Rd

Brighton Dam Office

Sundown Rd

Brighton Rd

Brighton Dam Rd

Greenbridge Rd

Georgia Ave

Zion Rd

97

Market St

New Hampshire Ave

650

BROOKEVILLE

Georgia Ave

Brookeville Rd

← Arrow shows direction of travel

Magruder Farm

Laytonsville Rd

108

Muncaster Rd

N

Muncaster Mill Rd

Redland Rd

0   1   2 mi.

0   1   2 km

(Shady Grove Metro Station)

M ★ Start/Finish

© The Countryman Press

wading are prohibited. (If you must wade, there's an inviting stretch of the Patuxent farther on.) Also remember that bike helmets are required by law for children 16 and under in both Howard and Montgomery Counties.

0.0 Exit the Shady Grove Metro station by the bus route and turn left onto Redland Road.

2.8 Cross Muncaster Mill Road.

You'll find fast food, shops, and gas stations. Redland Road continues as Muncaster Road.

6.7 Muncaster Road ends. Turn right onto Laytonsville Road (MD 108).

George's Liquor Store (right) has carryout food.

6.8 Taking care to avoid the traffic on Laytonsville Road, turn left onto Brookeville Road.

This is a pleasant 3-mile stretch past farms and woods.

9.8 Brookeville Road ends at Georgia Avenue (MD 97).

Bear right onto Georgia Avenue and follow it as it winds up a hill, past grand but unpretentious houses into the town of Brookeville.

10.0 At the top of the hill stands the post office (right).

After the British burned the White House, James and Dolley Madison found refuge near here on August 26, 1814, in the home of Brookeville postmaster Caleb Bentley.
Georgia Avenue turns right in front of the post office.
The tour goes straight, past the side of the post office, on Market Street.
Market Street takes you past more lovely homes. At the bottom of a hill, it leaves town and becomes Brighton Dam Road, which rolls up and down hills.

12.7 Turn left onto New Hampshire Avenue (MD 650).

This is not a major artery at this point, but watch for traffic.

13.1 Turn right onto Greenbridge Road.

Watch immediately on your left for the entrance to Catoctin Vineyards. Tours are available on weekends from noon to 5 PM (301-774-2310).

13.7 Enter the parking lot of the public boat launch and mooring facility.

Although there are no picnic tables, this is a great spot to rest and view the reservoir. When you've drunk in your fill of the scenery, double back to New Hampshire Avenue.

14.3 Turn left onto New Hampshire Avenue.

14.7 Turn left onto Brighton Dam Road, which is a series of roller-coaster hills.

15.9 Turn right into the parking lot of the Brighton Dam office and information center, which has exhibits about the dam and the surrounding area.

At the end of the parking lot is a soda machine. Steps lead down to a picnic area in the midst of lush, inviting lawns below the dam. There is a playground and room to fish and walk along the Patuxent River. Across Brighton Dam Road, along the part of the reservoir that spills into the dam, are some azalea gardens developed by dam employees. They are open daily from noon to 7 PM during blooming season.

After a respite, continue on Brighton Dam Road across the dam. Once across, the road begins a steady climb.

17.0 Turn left onto Nichols Drive.

18.1 Turn left onto Highland Road.

19.0 Turn left onto Triadelphia Mill Road.

This is an area of rolling hills and encroaching suburbia, with a few farm holdouts.

20.2 At the bottom of a hill, Triadelphia Mill Road runs into Greenbridge Road. For a rest by the reservoir, turn left onto Greenbridge Road, which soon turns into easily negotiable, hard-packed gravel.

20.6 You'll arrive at the Pig Tail boat-launching area, where the water juts into the land in the shape of a pig's tail.

This is a nice place to sit under the weeping willows that grow along the bank.

Double back on the same road and continue on the paved portion of Greenbridge Road.

21.1 Turn left onto Triadelphia Mill Road.

22.8 On the left side of the road is a pleasant picnic and boat-launch facility— your last chance to rest by the reservoir on this tour.

23.5 Triadelphia Mill Road ends. Turn right onto Triadelphia Road.

25.2 Make a sharp left onto Roxbury Road, a rural road lined by cornfields.

27.5 Cross Georgia Avenue (MD 97) carefully and turn left onto it, riding on the paved shoulder. Watch for traffic.

29.6 Turn right onto Jennings Chapel Road.

29.9 Turn left onto Howard Chapel Road.

This is a scenic and quiet road that runs through undeveloped parkland along the Patuxent River, which is really just a stream at this point. Watch for turtles crossing and for low-flying goldfinches.

30.4 The road crosses the Patuxent and re-enters Montgomery County.

The point where the road crosses the stream is a good fishing, wading, and resting spot. The road goes up a slight incline past a horse farm.

32.2 Cross New Hampshire Avenue (MD 650).

32.4 Turn right onto Sundown Road. Watch for traffic.

32.9 Turn left onto Zion Road.

This is a low-traffic road that leads past Mount Zion Church.

35.9 Turn right onto Brookeville Road. From now on, you'll be retracing the route you took at the beginning of the trip.

36.5 Turn right onto Laytonsville Road (MD 108).

36.6 Turn left onto Muncaster Road.

39.0 On a hill to your right stands the Magruder Farm.

Owned by the county, it's used to teach schoolchildren about the area's agricultural past. It started as a tobacco farm in 1734 and later became a wheat farm known as Waveland.

41.7 Cross Muncaster Mill Road. Muncaster Road continues as Redland Road.

By this time, you may be ready for some of the fast food available at this intersection.

44.0 Turn right into the Shady Grove Metro station parking lot.

Bicycle Repair Service

Griffin Cycle, Inc., 3494 Olney-Laytonsville Road, Olney, Maryland (301-774-3970)

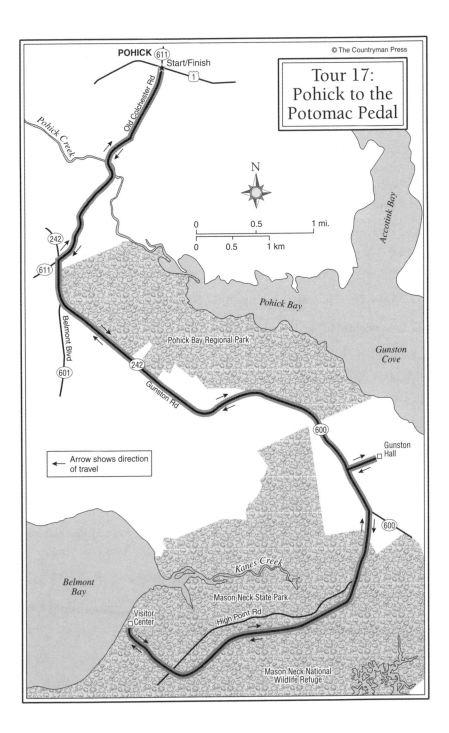

POHICK ⑥⑪
Start/Finish
①

© The Countryman Press

Tour 17:
Pohick to the
Potomac Pedal

Pohick Creek

Old Colchester Rd

N

0   0.5   1 mi.

0   0.5   1 km

Accotink Bay

②④②

⑥⑪

Belmont Blvd

⑥⓪①

Pohick Bay

Pohick Bay Regional Park

Gunston
Cove

②④②

Gunston Rd

Arrow shows direction
of travel

⑥⓪⓪

Gunston
Hall

⑥⓪⓪

Kanes Creek

Belmont
Bay

Mason Neck State Park

Visitor
Center

High Point Rd

Mason Neck National
Wildlife Refuge

17

Pohick to the Potomac Pedal

LOCATION: Fairfax County, Virginia

TERRAIN: Moderately hilly

ROAD CONDITIONS: Paved, light-traffic roads and a paved bicycle trail

DISTANCE: 18.6 miles

HIGHLIGHTS: The Old Pohick Church, Gunston Hall, Mason Neck State Park and National Wildlife Refuge

In a sense, this tour could be called "in the footsteps of George Mason," the behind-the-scenes statesman (1725–1792) who penned the Virginia Declaration of Rights, which helped inspire both our Bill of Rights and France's Declaration of the Rights of Man. The tour starts at the Old Pohick Church, where Mason, along with George Washington and Lord Fairfax, was a vestryman, visits his home Gunston Hall, and wanders through Mason Neck, formerly part of Mason's estate and now a state park and national wildlife refuge dedicated to nurturing the bald eagle—which flourished in Mason's time and is now making a comeback.

To get to the Old Pohick Church from the Beltway, take US 1 South, past Fort Belvoir to the intersection of US 1, Telegraph Road (VA 611), and Old Colchester Road in Lorton, Virginia. The church has a parking lot. Take time to tour the church, which is open daily. The present building was completed in 1774, and the Masons, the Washingtons, and other prominent local families bought pews. It's surrounded by boxwoods and a burying ground.

0.0 Exit the parking lot and turn right on Old Colchester Road (VA 611), following it down a hill and across Pohick Creek. The road runs through the Accotink

Bay Wildlife Refuge, past a pollution control plant and a few houses, then winds up a hill.

1.8 On your left, a road leads to the Tamarack Stables. On your right is the Cranford United Methodist Church. This was the original site of the Old Pohick Church.

1.9 At the intersection with Gunston Road (VA 242) stands the Old Country Store, an old-fashioned rural corner store that once had gas pumps under its portico. Local residents are trying to revitalize the store; plans call for an art gallery and a bakery.

Turn left on Gunston Road, which runs through farm country, passing Meadowood Wildlife Management Area and Pohick Bay Regional Park.

4.8 Turn left into Gunston Hall, following a road lined with alternating cedars and holly trees. To tour the house, outbuildings, and grounds, veer left at the V to the visitor center.

There is an admission charge, and tours are available daily. Highlights are the Chinese Chippendale dining room and the Palladian parlor, with intricate carved woodwork by an indentured English servant named William Buckland.

After your visit, double back on the entry road.

5.8 Turn left onto the paved bike path that parallels Gunston Road.

6.3 The path takes a right turn into Mason Neck State Park and National Wildlife Refuge. The wooded trail crosses several bridges. Watch for deer on the path.

9.8 The trail ends at a picnic area on the banks of Belmont Bay, an arm of the Potomac River.

Restrooms and a soda machine are available. Down a short road to the right is the nature center, which has a slide show and exhibits detailing the natural history of the area, once prime hunting and fishing grounds for the Dogue Indians. In the 19th and 20th centuries, loggers stripped the area of much of the pine and hardwoods, which led to a decline in the bald eagle population. Today, protection of the bald eagles—which have returned in encouraging numbers—is a prime purpose of the park. The fishermen have also returned, both in boats and along the shore. Here you'll find a beach to walk along and miles of hiking trails.

Boxwoods and a burial ground surround the Old Pohick Church, which dates from 1774.

After your visit, double back on the bike trail and follow it back to its terminus, near the entrance to Gunston Hall.

13.9 Exit the trail and continue along Gunston Road, which makes a very gradual climb.

16.7 Turn right on Old Colchester Road, which winds down a hill, then up again.

18.6 Turn left into the parking lot of the Old Pohick Church.

Bicycle Repair Service

Bikes USA, 14477 Potomac Mills Road, Woodbridge, Virginia (703-494-5300)

The Washington, Baltimore & Annapolis Trail

LOCATION: Prince George's County, Maryland

TERRAIN: Flat

ROAD CONDITIONS: Paved trail, shared with cars in places

DISTANCE: 11.6 miles

HIGHLIGHTS: A pleasant rail trail through suburban backyards and past horse farms, plus an optional side trip to the Marietta Manor Historic Site

Despite its rather grandiose name, this rail trail actually runs only 5.6 miles between Glenn Dale and Bowie, but, historically, it's part of a much bigger picture. While the railroad's main line ran parallel to the current Amtrak route, this segment rushed passengers from Washington to such then-rural communities as Glenn Dale and Bowie on state-of-the-art electric trains capable of speeds up to 70 mph. During racing season, extra trains ferried fans to Bowie Race Track. Plans are in the works to extend the trail across the Patuxent River to Odenton, where the old rail line connected to the South Shore line, which ran between Annapolis and Baltimore.

This tour starts at mile 1.0 of the trail, where it intersects with Glenn Dale Road. To get to the starting point, take the Baltimore Washington Parkway to MD 450 and head east. Just past the intersection with MD 704, keep left on MD 450 and go left again on Glenn Dale Road. Past the site of the old Glenn Dale Hospital, you'll see a small parking lot beside the trail on your right.

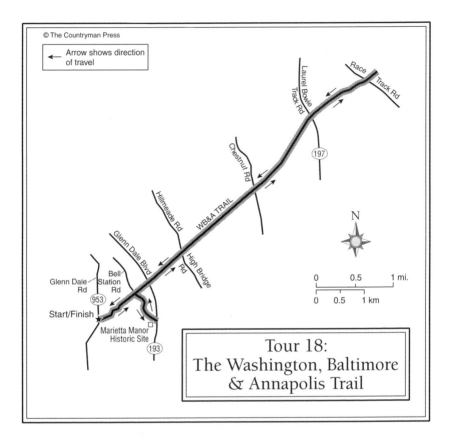

© The Countryman Press

Arrow shows direction of travel

Race Track Rd

Laurel Bowie Track Rd

Chestnut Rd

197

Hillmeade Rd

WB&A TRAIL

N

Glenn Dale Blvd

High Bridge Rd

0   0.5   1 mi.

0   0.5   1 km

Bell Station Rd

Glenn Dale Rd

953

Start/Finish

Marietta Manor Historic Site

193

Tour 18:
The Washington, Baltimore
& Annapolis Trail

0.0 Turn right onto the trail, which runs along Old Pond Road. The trail is shared with cars here, but there is little traffic .

On your right is a U.S. Depart ment of Agriculture Plant Introduction Center.

0.5 For an optional side trip to the Marietta Manor Historic Site, turn right on Bell Station Road and continue 0.6 mile to the two-and-a-half story gabled brick house built c. 1811 by Supreme Court Justice Gabriel Duvall.

The house is open for tours on some weekends, and it's pleasant to stroll around the box-wood-studded grounds. After your visit, reverse direction and return to the trail.

1.7 After crossing Bell Station Road, the trail turns left up a slight hill and becomes a pedestrian-cyclist-equestrian-only trail. Watch for horses and evidence of horses. The trail runs under power lines and is at least partially shaded.

Horses share the trail with cyclists and walkers (and dogs).

2.0 A tunnel takes the trail under MD 193.

3.6 A bridge takes the trail over Hillmeade Road and enters a section lined with ferns and honeysuckle.

3.9 Two bridges in a row take the trail over Highbridge Road and some railroad tracks and past a series of horse farms.

4.6 The Bowie Golf and Country Club is on your right.

5.1 The trail crosses MD 197 on a bridge and leads through a wooded area, some of which belongs to the Berwyn Gun Club. Signs warn cyclists to stay on the trail.

5.8 After tunneling under Race Track Road, the trail ends—temporarily, at least—in a parking lot. Reverse direction and retrace your steps.

11.6 Return to parking lot on Glenn Dale Road.

Bicycle Repair Service

A & M Cycles, 13002 9th Street, Bowie, Maryland (301-262-4343)

COUNTRY ROADS

Horses graze along a country road in Southern Maryland.

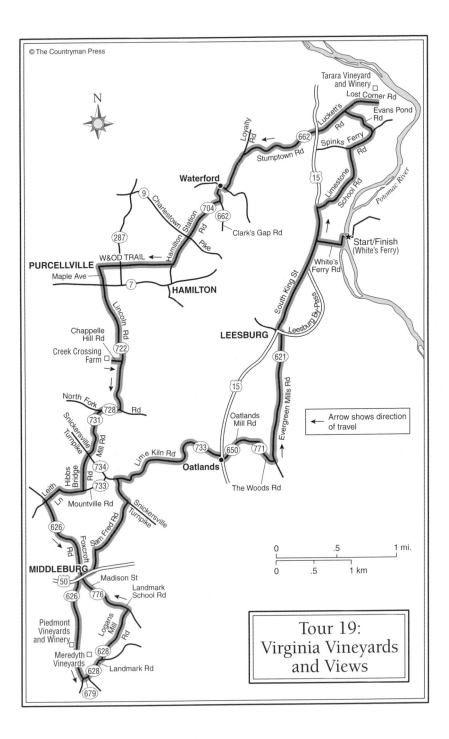

© The Countryman Press

N

Tarara Vineyard
and Winery
Lost Corner Rd
Evans Pond
Rd
Loyalty Rd
662
Luckett's Rd
Spinks Ferry Rd
Stumptown Rd
15
Limestone School Rd
Potomac River

Waterford
9
704
Charlestown Station Rd
662
Clark's Gap Rd
287
Hamilton Station Pike
15
Start/Finish
(White's Ferry)

W&OD TRAIL
PURCELLVILLE
Maple Ave
7
HAMILTON
White's Ferry Rd
South King St
Leesburg By-Pass

LEESBURG
621
Lincoln Rd
Chappelle Hill Rd
722
Creek Crossing Farm
15
Evergreen Mills Rd
North Fork Rd
728
731
Oatlands Mill Rd

Arrow shows direction
of travel

Snickersville Turnpike
Mill Rd
Lime Kiln Rd
733
650
771
Oatlands
734
Hibbs Bridge Rd
733
Leith Ln
Mountville Rd
Snickersville Turnpike
The Woods Rd
626
Sam Fred Rd
Foxcroft Rd

0   .5   1 mi.
0   .5   1 km

MIDDLEBURG
50
Madison St
626
776
Landmark School Rd
Piedmont Vineyards and Winery
Logans Mill Rd
628
Meredyth Vineyards
628
Landmark Rd
679

Tour 19:
Virginia Vineyards
and Views

19

Virginia Vineyards and Views

LOCATION: Montgomery County in Maryland, and Loudoun and Fauquier Counties in Virginia

TERRAIN: Hilly

ROAD CONDITIONS: Paved and dirt-and-gravel roads and a paved bike trail

DISTANCE: 77.6 miles

HIGHLIGHTS: The "lost corner" of Virginia, vineyards, the Quaker villages of Waterford and Lincoln, the Washington and Old Dominion Railroad Trail, Middleburg and surrounding horse country, historic Leesburg

The first day of this trip begins with a ride across the Potomac on an old-fashioned cable ferry and then goes even deeper into the past. After exploring the rural "lost corner" of Virgina and visiting a winery, it winds to the landmark village of Waterford, settled by Pennsylvania Quakers in 1773 and christened by an Irish settler named Thomas Moore a few years later. The tour then makes its way to the Washington and Old Dominion Railroad Trail, then turns south to another Quaker town, Lincoln, for an overnight at a charming and hospitable farm bed & breakfast inn. The next day, the tour makes its way through posh horse country to Middleburg, mecca for the horsey set. After a stop there and an optional loop that takes you to two wineries, the tour follows beautiful Goose Creek along bucolic country roads to Leesburg, which was founded in 1758 and served as the nation's capital for a few days during the War of 1812. From downtown Leesburg, with its wide choice of restaurants and antiques shops, it's a short hop back to the ferry.

An abbreviated version of this trip could be done in a day if you return to Leesburg on the bike trail after mile 23.3. From this point, it's an easy 6.5 miles to Leesburg and another 4.4 miles to the ferry. You can also shorten the trip by skipping the optional loop to the Piedmont and Meredyth Vineyards from Middleburg.

To get to White's Ferry from the Beltway, take I-270 to the MD 28 exit and follow MD 28 in the direction of Darnestown. Continue to Dawsonville and turn left onto White's Ferry Road (MD 107). The ferry is at the end of the road and runs year-round, seven days a week, from 5 AM until well past dark. During unusually high water, the ferry may not be able to cross. For information, call 301-349-5200. The ferry has a large parking lot and a store.

DAY 1

0.0 Ride off the ferry on the Virginia shore, following White's Ferry Road, which is lined with wild bluebells in spring.

1.2 Turn right onto US 15N, riding on the shoulder.

2.6 Turn right onto Limestone School Road, which is hard-packed dirt and gravel with little traffic. It winds through woods and past farms.

On your left is the entrance to Temple Hall Farm Regional Park, an outdoor education facility for school groups that is open to the general public only on special occasions. (Call 703-729-0596 for information.) The pleasant manor house was built around 1810 by a nephew of George Mason, author of Virginia's Declaration of Rights (see Tour 17). It was restored by the Symington family in the 1940s and donated to the park authority in 1985. It showcases Virginia's farming heritage and houses many farm animals, including goats, pigs, and sheep.

Continue on Limestone School Road, which affords views of Maryland's Sugarloaf Mountain to your right and passes large horse farms.

6.3 Turn right onto Spinks Ferry Road, which is also dirt and gravel. You are now in Virginia's "lost corner," a rural area of farms and country homes high above the Potomac River.

7.6 Turn left onto Evans Pond Road, which is paved.

9.1 Turn right onto Lucketts Road (VA 662).

This road is a ribbon through a broad agricultural valley rimmed by blue mountains.

9.7 Lucketts Road becomes Lost Corner Road and bears right, through a small settlement and past vineyards.

10.6 Turn left into Tarara (Ararat spelled backward) Vineyard and Winery.
The winery offers tours Thursday through Monday 11 AM–5 PM. The 60-acre site overlooks the Potomac and produces chardonnays, cabernets, and other fine wines.

After your tour, reverse direction on Lost Corner Road.

11.5 Lost Corner Road becomes Lucketts Road.

13.6 Lucketts Road crosses US 15.
At the intersection are several antiques shops and a gas station. Past the intersection, Lucketts Road becomes Stumptown Road, which winds mainly uphill but affords some exhilarating downhill runs.

17.2 Turn left onto Loyalty Road, which leads into Waterford. Bear left onto Water Street (VA 698), then turn right onto Main Street.
Pennsylvania Quakers settled Waterford in 1773, but the town got its name a few years later when Irish settler Thomas Moore persuaded his neighbors to call the growing village after his hometown back in Ireland. Waterford served the surrounding farms, providing such services as milling, tanning, and coachmaking. The entire village is now a National Historic Landmark. Many of the historic homes are open for tours on one weekend in October. Contact the Waterford Foundation (703-882-3018) for information and for a map to use for walking tours, or pick one up at any of the shops. Of particular interest are the mill, the weaver's cottage, the tin shop, the Second Street School, and the jail.

19.2 At the post office, make a sharp left onto 2nd Street, which curves past more beautiful homes and becomes Factory Street.

19.3 Turn right onto Clarks Gap Road (VA 662), which is busy.

19.9 Turn right onto Hamilton Station Road (VA 704).
The road winds mainly uphill past farms and posh new homes. The road crosses Charles Town Pike (VA 9) and ends at the defunct Hamilton station on the Washington and Old Dominion. Trains once brought Washingtonians to this station for summer respites in the Quaker hamlet of Hamilton.

23.3 Turn right onto the W&OD Trail, which is wooded on both sides.
Watch for cattle, which sometimes wander close to get a better view of the action.

Creek Crossing Farm, a working farm with a restored 1773 house, offers bed and breakfast to cyclists and others.

25.4 The trail emerges from the woods and seems to end, but it doesn't. Follow the marked path along VA 287, crossing at the crosswalk and continuing on the trail toward Purcellville.

26.6 Exit the trail at Maple Avenue, bearing left, past a firehouse and some fast-food establishments. Cross VA 7 (Business) at the light, after which Maple Avenue becomes Lincoln Road (VA 722).

Follow Lincoln Road through a pleasant residential area and into the country.

28.0 After passing through the small Quaker settlement of Lincoln, turn right onto Chappelle Hill Road.

28.1 Take the first farm entrance into Creek Crossing Farm.

The farm offers bed & breakfast on a 20-acre farm (see Accommodations). The restored 18th-century farmhouse sits on a hill and is furnished with antiques. After a refreshing night at the inn, the tour continues on to Middleburg.

DAY 2

28.2 After leaving the B&B, turn left onto Chappelle Hill Road and right onto Lincoln Road.

31.6 Turn right onto North Fork Road (VA 728).

32.3 Turn left onto Mill Road (VA 731), looking to your right for sweeping mountain views.

34.4 Turn left onto Snickersville Turnpike (VA 734), which leads downhill and across a bridge.

34.5 Turn right onto Hibbs Bridge Road, which is hard-packed dirt and gravel but very scenic, running through woods above a stream.

35.9 Turn right onto Mountville Road (VA 733), which is paved.

37.0 Bear left onto Leith Lane.

37.8 Turn left onto Foxcroft Road (VA 626), which winds its way up and down hills past the posh horse farms that Middleburg is famous for.

40.3 On your left is Glenwood Park, a public park that hosts point-to-point steeplechase races accompanied by elegant tailgate picnics in spring and fall.

41.6 Foxcroft Road ends. Bear right at Mosby's Tavern.

This popular restaurant and watering hole was named for Colonel John Mosby, the Confederate irregular who operated hereabouts. At the tavern, turn left onto Madison Street. On your right is the Pink Box, an information center staffed by helpful volunteers. Restrooms are available, and there's a beautiful garden dedicated to Jacqueline Kennedy, who used to ride in the Middleburg area.

Middleburg dates from 1731, when a cousin of George Washington opened a tavern on Ashby's Gap Turnpike. The turnpike is now known as US 50 and the tavern as the Red Fox. Today Middleburg is the site of multimillion-dollar horse farms and a few wineries.

Horse farms welcome the public only once a year, usually Memorial Day weekend, in a stable tour that benefits Trinity Episcopal Church in nearby Upperville.

For a dining alternative to Mosby's Tavern and the Red Fox Inn, turn right at the intersection of US 50 and go one block to the Upper Crust Bakery, which offers delicious sandwiches and freshly baked pies and cookies. Outdoor tables are available.

After your meal, reverse direction on US 50. To skip the optional loop to the wineries, continue east on this road and pick up the rest of the tour at mile 52.8.

42.5 If you wish to visit two local wineries, turn right onto VA 626. You'll climb and descend some hills and pass large estates with horse pastures protected by stone fences.

45.3 Turn right into Piedmont Vineyards and Winery.

Pass the sign requesting DO NOT BOTHER SWANS and the mellow, yellow Waverly, a landmark pre–Revolutionary War mansion and residence of the Furness family, which founded the vineyard in 1973. Although Virginians, including Thomas Jefferson, had long sought to establish wineries, this was the first commercial vinifera vineyard in the state. The 36-acre vineyard is planted with chardonnay, semillon, and seyval blanc grapes.

45.5 Park at the old dairy barn that now houses the winery and sales room.

It's open Tuesday through Sunday 10 AM–4 PM. Tours and tastings are informal and free. A guide will walk you through the wine-making process and show you the machines that press the grapes, the stainless-steel tanks where the juice, or "must," is placed in order to allow the suspended solid matter to settle out, and the temperature-controlled oak fermenting barrels. Piedmont produces about seven thousand cases of wine a year. The output includes two chardonnays, a semillon, and two white wines made from the seyval blanc grape. Little River White is semidry, and Hunt Country White is dry. You'll be invited to taste several wines, and you'll probably want to buy a bottle for your picnic. Since biking and drinking aren't compatible, go easy on the tasting.

Just outside the winery are picnic tables. As you picnic with Waverly as a backdrop, don't be surprised to have horses looking over your shoulder.

After the tour, continue south on VA 626.

45.9 Turn left onto VA 679 (not well marked; easy to miss).

46.0 VA 679 ends. Bear left onto VA 628 (Landmark Road).

47.1 VA 628 meets VA 686 at a V. Bear left, remaining on VA 628 (Logans Mill Road).

47.4 Take a left at the Meredyth Vineyards sign and follow the dirt road.

The road leads through the 56-acre vineyard, set against the spectacular backdrop of the Bull Run Mountains. On your way in, you'll come to some picturesque picnic grounds, complete with ruins of old stone buildings, but you may want to wait until you've taken the tour and purchased some wine.

47.8 Park in front of the winery, a large green barn.

Tours are available daily 10 AM–4 PM (except Christmas, Easter, Thanksgiving, and New Year's Day). Meredyth produces an impressive variety of wines, including seyval blanc, villard blanc, riesling, chardonnay, cabernet sauvignon, and merlot, from its French-American hybrids, and the winery puts on a good tour.

48.2 Exit the vineyard and go left onto VA 628.

The road is loosely packed gravel with lots of hills.

50.2 Turn left onto VA 776 (Landmark School Road). This runs into Madison Street in Middleburg.

52.8 Turn right onto US 50.

53.5 At St. Stephen's Catholic Church, turn left onto Sam Fred Road (VA 748), which rolls through wooded hills.

56.9 Sam Fred Road ends at Cotswald Farm, a major horse farm. Turn left onto Snickersville Turnpike (VA 734).

58.0 At the T, turn right onto Lime Kiln Road (VA 733).

The road turns to dirt and gravel and winds through picturesque woods and farmland beside Goose Creek.

61.5 Pavement resumes and the road gets wider.

63.6 Lime Kiln Road ends in the small crossroads of Oatlands, at US 15.

Note: The mansion of the same name is not right here, and you would have an unpleasant ride on busy US 15 to reach it.

Cross US 15 and ride on the shoulder past the Episcopal Church of Our Savior.

63.7 Turn left onto Oatlands Mill Road (VA 650), also a picturesque rural dirt road.

65.1 At the crossroads, continue straight on The Woods Road (VA 771).
The road winds uphill through deep woods, and there are some rough patches of gravel.

66.9 The Woods Road ends on Evergreen Mill Road (VA 621). Turn left onto this paved road leading through increasingly suburban areas into Leesburg.

72.1 Evergreen Mill Road ends at South King Street. Turn right onto South King Street, taking care to avoid the cars that are turning in to the Leesburg Bypass.

73.2 South King Street crosses the W&OD bike trail and leads into downtown Leesburg.
Founded in 1758 and named for Light Horse Harry Lee, the town served as the nation's capital for a few days during the War of 1812: the Constitution and the Declaration of Independence were brought here for safekeeping. The picturesque mellow, red-brick town offers a variety of antiques shops and eating places.

After a respite, continue up South King Street (US 15 Business). Be careful when it rejoins US 15 and ride on the shoulder.

76.4 Turn right onto White's Ferry Road.

77.6 Ride onto the ferry and cross the Potomac, returning to the parking lot.

Bicycle Repair Service

Bicycle Outfitters, 19 Catoctin Circle NE, Leesburg, Virginia (703-777-6126)

Accommodations

Creek Crossing Farm at Chappelle Hill, Lincoln, Virginia (540-338-7550)

20

Cruising around Croom

LOCATION: Prince George's County, Maryland

TERRAIN: Almost flat

ROAD CONDITIONS: Park roads and country roads with light traffic

DISTANCE: 28.5 miles

HIGHLIGHTS: Patuxent River Park, Merkle Wildlife Sanctuary, St. Thomas Church

This tour takes you to a part of Maryland's Prince George's County that's still country—a place where tobacco still grows, osprey still nest, and where the Canada geese come to eat the wild rice and end up staying the winter. The tour begins at Patuxent River Park, where the Patuxent River widens into Jug Bay. Following the Chesapeake Bay Critical Areas Drive, the tour visits the first airfield in the United States owned and operated by an African American and stops at an observation tower over a tidal marsh. After a stop at St. Thomas Church, completed in 1745, the tour takes in Merkle Wildlife Sanctuary and Visitor Center, which hosts hummingbirds and Canada geese, and continues to now nonexistent Nottingham, a hotbed of intrigue and activity during the War of 1812. After a look at Mattaponi, built in 1745 by the Bowie family, the trip ends back in Patuxent River Park.

To get to Patuxent River Park from the Beltway, take MD 4 to US 301 south. Take US 301 to Croom Road (MD 382), then take Croom Road south to Croom Airport Road. Turn left onto Croom Airport Road and continue to the park entrance. Leave your car in the lot near the park office.

Either before or after your bike ride, you'll want to enjoy some of the attractions of this 2,000-acre park—by taking a stroll on the boardwalk

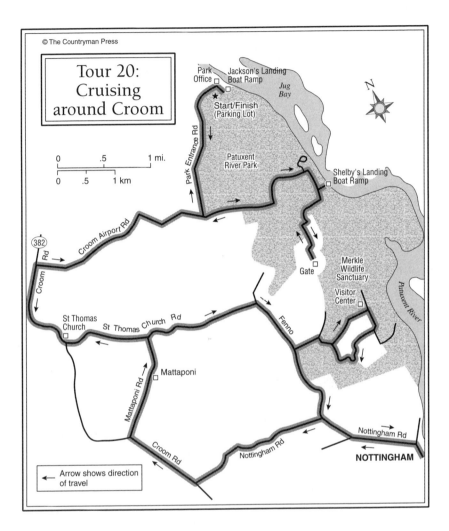

© The Countryman Press

Tour 20: Cruising around Croom

0   .5   1 mi.

0   .5   1 km

that leads through the wetlands and by touring the Patuxent village, an exhibit that depicts life on the river in the 19th century. Check at the park office for a schedule of events. By calling ahead (301-627-6094), you may be able to make arrangements for canoeing or camping or for a ride on an electric boat.

0.0 Exit the parking lot and head back out the park entrance road.

1.7 Turn left onto Croom Airport Road, which winds to the left down a hill.

2.4 At the bottom of the hill, turn left, following the signs for Selby's Landing Boat Ramp.

3.1 A sign in a field marks the site of the Columbia Air Center.

The first airfield owned and operated by an African American, it was opened in 1941 by John W. Greene Jr. During World War II, the Navy used the field for training.

3.7 Selby's Landing Boat Ramp has a dock if you want to sit by the river.

4.8 The road turns to a wooden bridge over a freshwater tidal marsh.

An observation tower allows you to watch for the birds, muskrats, and diamondback terrapin that frequent the marsh. Serious birders sometimes set up telescopes on the bridge. They appreciate quiet. On the other side of the bridge is Merkle Wildlife Sanctuary. Dirt roads lead to the visitor center, but bicycles are not allowed on them except during specified times. Currently, cyclists and hikers may use this route on summer Saturdays 10 AM–3 PM. Call 301-888-1410 for up-to-date information.

Otherwise, you need to backtrack to the entrance of Patuxent River Park on Croom Airport Road.

7.9 At the park entrance, continue on Croom Airport Road.

9.9 Turn left onto Croom Road.

10.8 Turn left onto St. Thomas Church Road.

On your left, immediately after the turn, is the church, completed in 1745 but with Victorian alterations. In the churchyard, among the pines and cedars, are graves of some of the first families of Maryland: Bowies and Calverts and Duvalls. There is also a memorial to a former rector, Thomas John Claggett, who later became the first Episcopalian bishop consecrated in the United States. Inscribed on the memorial is a quote from Claggett: "How awesome is the dawn sky over the hills of Croom . . . It makes my heart sing 'praised be God.' "

13.2 Turn right onto Fenno Road.

This is a rural road that parallels the river.

13.9 Turn left into Merkle Wildlife Sanctuary and follow the one-way loop to the visitor center.

Merkle was a local farmer and wildlife lover who donated this property for conservation purposes. The center is open 10 AM–4 PM, Tuesday through Sunday, and has exhibits on the river and the animals found in its watershed. A special feature is a hummingbird garden with telescopes set up so you can view the tiny birds at close range. There is also a pond favored by visiting waterfowl.

After your visit, return to Fenno Road, completing the one-way loop.

15.7 Turn left onto Fenno Road.

17.6 Turn left onto Nottingham Road.

This road ends at the river, but with no access. Nottingham, which now consists of only a few houses, was once a thriving port. During the War of 1812, it served as headquarters for Commodore Joshua Barney, whose flotilla was bottled up here by the British fleet. Secretary of State James Monroe reportedly donned cloak and dagger and came to Nottingham to size up the British forces, who were advancing up the Patuxent and camped in Nottingham the night of August 21, 1814 (See also Tour 23).

Turn around and backtrack on Nottingham Road, continuing past the intersection with Fenno Road, through tobacco-farming country.

20.7 Turn right onto Croom Road (MD 382).

21.6 Turn right onto Mattaponi Road.

22.3 Mattaponi, built around 1745, is on your right.

The two-and-a-half-story hip-roofed house was once the ancestral home of the Bowies, some of whom are buried in St. Thomas churchyard. Today, it's owned by the Catholic Church.

22.8 Turn left onto St. Thomas Church Road and follow it up a small hill, past the church.

23.7 Turn right onto Croom Road.

24.8 Turn right onto Croom Airport Road.

26.8 Turn left into Patuxent River Park.

28.5 Return to the parking lot.

Bicycle Repair Service

Mike's Bikes of Waldorf, 2102 Crain Highway, Waldorf, Maryland (301-870-6600)

21

Getaway to Galesville

LOCATION: Prince George's and Anne Arundel Counties in Maryland

METRO ACCESS: New Carrollton

TERRAIN: Rolling to moderately hilly

ROAD CONDITIONS: Paved roads, most with little traffic

DISTANCE: 51.4 miles

HIGHLIGHTS: Historic churches; the Old Quaker Burying Ground; Galesville, with its restaurants, antiques shops, and waterfront parks

Galesville, long a popular boating destination for Washingtonians, also makes a good bike-trip destination. It's probably the nearest Chesapeake Bay town to Washington—although it's actually on the West River near the point where the river joins the bay.

Established in 1684, Galesville was an active port during the steamboat era. Today it is a stately old town with large frame houses lining the main street. Its economy is based on an oyster cannery, plus a lot of businesses that serve visiting boaters, including marinas and restaurants. What makes the town a nice place to visit is that some of its waterfront has been set aside as parkland, making it available for picnicking.

The tour starts at the New Carrollton Metro station, terminus of the Orange Line, and quickly takes the rider into the country.

0.0 Exit the New Carrollton station on the east side, following the bus lane. At the exit, turn right onto Garden City Drive, then left at the V, under US 50. Continue to the left onto Ardwick Ardmore Road.

At first the road is lined with factories and other light industries, but it soon turns more countrylike.

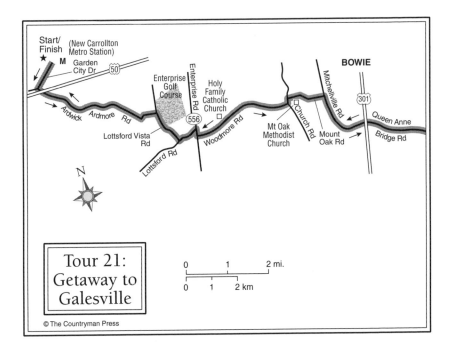

3.3 Ardwick Ardmore Road ends in front of the Enterprise Golf Course. Turn right onto Lottsford Vista Road.

4.5 Lottsford Vista Road ends. Turn left onto Lottsford Road.

5.2 Lottsford Road ends at Enterprise Road (MD 556). Cross Enterprise Road—carefully—and continue straight ahead on Woodmore Road.

5.7 The white-clapboard Holy Family Catholic Church, set amid tall trees, dates from 1890.

8.1 Woodmore Road ends at Church Road. On your right is the Mount Oak Methodist Church Cemetery, established in 1890. Turn left onto Church Road, then make an immediate right onto Mount Oak Road.

On your left, just after the turn, is the Mount Oak Methodist Church, built in 1881. The road continues over rolling hills in a country setting.

9.8 Turn right onto Mitchellville Road after stopping at the shopping center at the intersection for food if desired.

You have re-entered suburbia, the greater Bowie area.

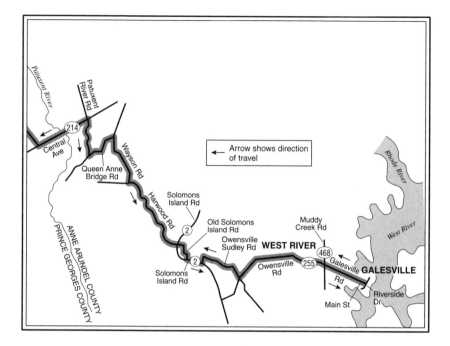

11.1 Proceed carefully across US 301 and its large center island. At the other side of the highway, Mitchellville Road becomes Queen Anne Bridge Road.

After a brief uphill climb, the road rolls through a pleasant rural area.

13.2 Turn left onto Central Avenue (MD 214). Watch for traffic.

After crossing the Patuxent River, you'll enter Anne Arundel County.

14.5 Turn right onto Patuxent River Road.

15.4 Turn left onto Queen Anne Bridge Road.

16.6 Make a sright onto Wayson Road in front of the National Guard installation.

This stretch features roller-coaster hills.

17.9 Turn left onto Harwood Road, which runs through cornfields and crosses shady Stocketts Run.

20.3 Cross Solomons Island Road (MD 2) at Harwood Post Office. Enter Old Solomons Island Road.

This is a rural loop that will minimize the time you have to spend on busy MD 2.

20.8 Old Solomons Island Road ends. Turn left onto Solomons Island Road (MD 2). Ride on the shoulder.

21.0 Turn left onto Owensville Sudley Road, which soon makes a right turn and travels through farm country.

22.3 Turn left onto Owensville Road (MD 255).

Christ Church Parish Hall, at the intersection, has a big front yard with a towering oak to rest under. Next door is the Episcopal church itself, a white frame structure with a boxwood-scented cemetery.

Leaving the town of West River, Owensville Road winds mainly downhill past tobacco farms and their weathered gray barns. The vertical slats on the barns slant open to allow air-drying of the hanging tobacco leaves.

24.7 Owensville Road crosses Muddy Creek Road (MD 468) and becomes Galesville Road.

On your right, just before the intersection, is a gas station and convenience store. Across the intersection lies the Old Quaker Burying Ground, founded in 1672, which may be explored through a gate in the picket fence, if you have the time and the inclination. A Quaker meetinghouse that once stood here burned during the Civil War.

25.5 R&M Antiques (left) is chock-full of china, bric-a-brac, and other old things.

25.6 You arrive at the West River Market & Deli on your left.

The market has groceries and excellent carryout sandwiches, and the building also houses a gift and antiques shop. There are picnic tables in the yard, but you may want to bring your sandwiches down to the waterfront. Next door to the market are two art galleries, and across the road is a marker showing that William Penn passed this way to board a boat across the Chesapeake.

25.7 The road meets the waterfront, where there is a small park.

You may picnic here, or try one of Galesville's several restaurants, all of which feature seafood. The Topside Inn is on the left at the intersection of MD 255 and Riverside Drive. A few hundred yards to the right is Steamboat Landing, a restaurant set on pilings in the river. It offers informal outdoor dining and will also arrange boat rides. Turn left onto Riverside Drive to Pirates Cove (right), which offers both food and lodging. Just past Pirates Cove, sandwiched between a marina and the West River Sailing Club, stands narrow Elizabeth Dixon Park, which features two picnic tables under a tree by the water. When you finish admiring the view of the West and Rhode Rivers flowing into Chesa-

An antiques store is a good place to rest and browse on the way to Galesville.

peake Bay, read the poem by Elizabeth Dixon that's engraved on a plaque set in a rock. A sampling reads: "Even the sun has a broken path/As it glistens across the sea./But the bright spot in the path it seems/Is always the furthest from me."

You should linger awhile in Galesville, boat-watching from the deck of the Steamboat Landing Restaurant as you sip a bloody mary with Old Bay seasoning dusted around the rim of the glass. You could dine here on crabs or other local fare, and spend the night—either in the Inn at Pirates Cove (301-261-5050) or at Oakwood, an 1840 manor house that now offers bed & breakfast (301-261-5338). If you must get back to Washington, however, you'll *have to cut short your visit to get home before dark. Although alternative routes were explored, none are recommended, so you'll have to reverse direction.*

29.1 Turn right onto Owensville Sudley Road.

30.4 Turn right onto MD 2 (Solomons Island Road).

30.6 Turn right onto Old Solomons Island Road.

31.1 Old Solomons Island Road ends. Cross MD 2 and enter Harwood Road.

33.5 Turn right onto Wayson Road.

34.8 Turn left onto Queen Anne Bridge Road.

36.0 Turn right onto Patuxent River Road.

36.9 Turn left onto MD 214. Watch for traffic.

38.2 Turn right onto Queen Anne Bridge Road.

40.3 After you cross US 301, Queen Anne Bridge Road becomes Mitchellville Road. Continue on Mitchellville Road.

41.6 Turn left onto Mount Oak Road.

43.2 Turn left onto Church Road, then make an immediate right onto Woodmore Road.

46.2 Cross Enterprise Road. Woodmore Road becomes Lottsford Road.

46.9 Turn right onto Lottsford Vista Road.

48.1 Turn left onto Ardwick Ardmore Road.

51.1 Following the "M" for Metro signs, turn left onto Pennsy Drive and cross the bridge.

51.3 Turn left onto Corporate Drive.

51.4 Arrive at New Carrollton Metro station.

Bicycle Repair Service

A&M Cycle, 13002 9th Street, Bowie, Maryland (301-262-4343)

22

Pedaling around Port Tobacco

LOCATION: Charles County, Maryland

TERRAIN: Rolling hills, with some flat stretches

ROAD CONDITIONS: Paved country roads with light traffic

DISTANCE: 12.4 miles

HIGHLIGHTS: St. Ignatius Roman Catholic Church and cemetery, Chapel Point State Park, Port Tobacco courthouse and museum, the Thomas Stone National Historic Site

The ghost town of Port Tobacco provides a glimpse into Maryland's 18th-century past—when tobacco was king, rivers were roads, and life revolved around gracious plantation homes, many of which are still standing. Founded on the site of an Indian village with a name that sounded like Potobac to the first European settlers, the town soon lived up to its name, shipping out hogsheads of tobacco on ships that sailed in and out of the port. The economy, based on slave labor, supported lavish plantations. When the Civil War took away both soldiers and slaves, the area began to decline. Nature also contributed to the town's demise when the river silted up, stranding the old port. A debate over moving the courthouse west to La Plata, which was served by the railroad, was settled in 1891 when the Port Tobacco courthouse "mysteriously" burned down. The arsonists had thoughtfully moved the records outside, and they were later transferred to La Plata, now the county seat.

Although deserted, the town is not gloomy. You can tour the restored courthouse and museum and one of the few remaining houses. You can also inspect St. Ignatius Church and its cemetery, wander the beach along the river, and look at the historic manor houses of Rose Hill from the road or at Habre de Venture, from closer up.

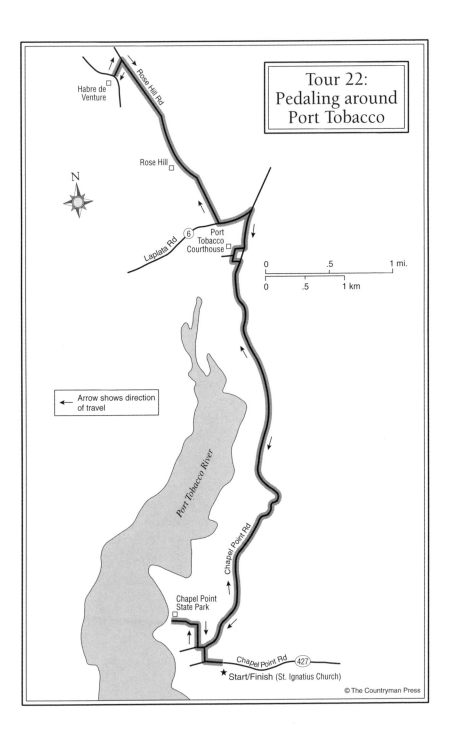

Tour 22:
Pedaling around
Port Tobacco

Habre de Venture

Rose Hill Rd

Rose Hill

N

Laplata Rd

6

Port Tobacco Courthouse

0   .5   1 mi.

0   .5   1 km

Arrow shows direction of travel

Port Tobacco River

Chapel Point Rd

Chapel Point State Park

Chapel Point Rd   427

★ Start/Finish (St. Ignatius Church)

© The Countryman Press

Start your tour at St. Ignatius Roman Catholic Church, Chapel Point, which has a parking lot. To reach the starting point from the Beltway, take MD 5 south to US 301. Take US 301 south through La Plata to the intersection with MD 427 (Chapel Point Road). Turn right onto Chapel Point Road to the church.

0.0 From St. Ignatius, continue west on Chapel Point Road, down a short, steep hill, and around a sharp curve.

Rosy redbrick St. Ignatius Church was built in 1789 on the site of a chapel built by Father Andrew White, who sailed into Maryland with the first group of settlers in 1634. The adjacent manor house, which dates from 1741, was built on the site of an earlier home. It has been occupied since then by Jesuits, many of whom are buried in the nearby graveyard. The graveyard, which slopes down toward the river, is a peaceful place that affords an unsurpassed view of the river, the lush countryside, and, on a hill up the river, Rose Hill, once the home of one of George Washington's doctors.

0.5 Take a left at the sign into Chapel Point State Park. The road will curve right, then left to the river, a parking lot, and a pebbly beach.

The sign says NO SWIMMING but fishing is allowed, and you can wander along the beach and at least wade. Past the duck blind to your left there's a shady picnic site.

Retrace your steps to the entrance to the park.

0.9 Turn left at the park exit onto Chapel Point Road.

This slightly rolling road leads past tobacco farms, woods, and a few suburban-type dwellings.

4.8 At the historical marker, turn left into the old courthouse square.

Most of the homes around the square, with 18th-century dates on them, are privately owned and inhabited. After securing your bike, however, you can visit the restored courthouse and museum for a nominal fee. It's open June through August, Wednesday through Sunday from noon to 4 PM, and April, May, and September through December, weekends from noon to 4 PM. The museum contains a mock-up of the large settlement, including hotels and tobacco warehouses that once thrived here, as well as gleanings from an archaeological dig. The entrance fee also covers a 30-minute video and a visit to the "catslide" house, built in 1700 and named for its steep roof. Tobacco grows in a neighboring plot. There is also a picnic table and a well of fresh water for filling water bottles.

After your visit, return to Chapel Point Road and turn left.

5.2 Turn left onto MD 6.

At the intersection with MD 6 stands Murphy's (left), a store offering liquor and groceries. You can sit at picnic tables outside and order barbecued ribs cooked in a pit on the grounds.

5.5 Turn right onto Rose Hill Road, which climbs a steep hill.

6.2 Take a left onto the dirt road (driveway) to Habre de Venture, the Thomas Stone National Historic Site. It's open Wednesday through Sunday 9 AM–5 PM.

Built by Thomas Stone, a signer of the Declaration of Independence, the house is architecturally unusual. Its hip-roofed central building and two wings form a crescent. Stone is buried on the grounds; you can see his grave from the dirt road that leads to the house.

After your visit, reverse direction, backtracking down Rose Hill Road.

6.9 Turn left onto Laplata Road (MD 6).

7.2 Turn right onto Chapel Point Road.

12.3 Follow Chapel Point Road around a sharp, uphill curve.

12.4 Return to St. Ignatius.

Bicycle Repair Service

Mike's Bikes of Waldorf, 2102 Crain Highway, Waldorf, Maryland (301-870-6600)

23

Biking the British Invasion Route

LOCATION: Calvert and Charles Counties, Maryland

TERRAIN: Moderately hilly

ROAD CONDITIONS: Paved country road

DISTANCE: 17.4 or 34.8 miles

HIGHLIGHTS: Jefferson Patterson Park, Battle Creek Cypress Swamp and Nature Center, the waterfront town of Benedict

In the summer of 1814, Washington girded for an invasion by its former masters. Knowing that the fledgling nation's capital would be a feather in the cap of the British, the U.S. built forts along the Potomac to foil the British fleet. Instead, the British sailed up the unfortified Patuxent River. Commodore Joshua Barney, a Revolutionary War hero turned privateer, persuaded the young government to finance a fleet of shallow-draft, oar-powered barges, which he and his fellow volunteers manned to harass the more powerful British fleet. After a first battle, the Americans retreated into St. Leonard Creek, which was too shallow for the bigger British boats. Blockading the mouth of the creek, the Brits tried to lure the Americans out by burning tobacco warehouses and plantations along the river. But the Americans stayed put, and U.S. artillery forces gathered on a bluff overlooking the mouth of the creek and turned heavy guns on the British fleet while Barney's forces attacked from the barges. Some of the ships sank in the battle, and underwater archaeologists have recovered many artifacts. Alas, the Battle of St. Leonard Creek served only to delay the British fleet, which continued up the Patuxent, landed at Benedict, marched overland to fight a victorious battle at Bladensburg, and then marched into Washington

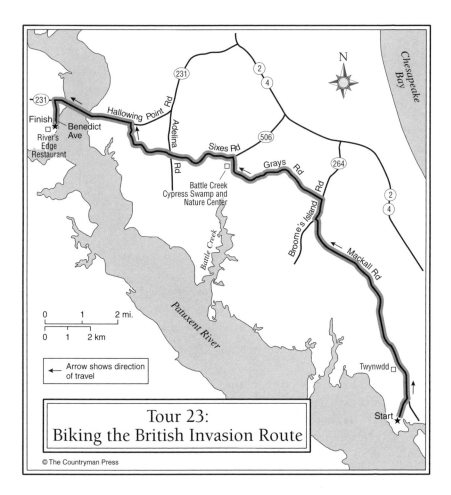

Tour 23:
Biking the British Invasion Route

© The Countryman Press

to burn the Capitol, the White House, and the Treasury. Only a sudden
summer storm prevented more widespread destruction.

This tour starts in Jefferson Patterson Park (open April 15–Oct. 15),
near the site of the Battle of St. Leonard Creek and follows the route
the British might have taken to Benedict if they had been on bicycles
rather than boats. To get to Jefferson Patterson Park, take Beltway
exit 11A and continue south on MD 4 past Prince Frederick. Turn right
on Broome's Island Road (MD 264) and left on Mackall Road (MD 265).
Park entrance is at the end of Mackall Road. Continue to the last parking lot, where there is signage about the Battle of St. Leonard Creek.

As this was only a one-way trip for the British, you might want to shuttle a car to Benedict and park at one of the waterfront restaurants, such as The River's Edge Restaurant.

0.0 Bike north along the park road, under an avenue of cedars, with a magnificent view of the Patuxent River on your left. On your right is the Maryland Archeological Conservation Laboratory, which houses some of the artifacts recovered from the Battle of St. Leonard Creek. (Free tours are conducted the first Friday of every month; call 410-535-4583.)

0.5 A walking trail to the left leads to the site of King's Reach, a plantation dating from the early 1700s, which has been partially excavated.

1.2 Exit the park and turn left onto Mackall Road, continuing past a series of horse farms.

1.9 On your left stands Tynnewdd, built in 1782, one of the river plantations not destroyed by the British. After passing the mansion and a large farm, look to your left for a glimpse of the Patuxent. On your right, you will pass two large tobacco barns.

Long vertical doors let in air to dry the tobacco, which was hung from the rafters. A few years ago, most tobacco farmers accepted a state buyout and switched to other crops. Southern Maryland's tobacco barns are now on the National Trust for Historic Preservation's Most Endangered Places list.

3.9 After passing another tobacco barn (right), cross Parran Road and continue on Mackall Road.

6.7 Turn right onto Broome's Island Road.

7.2 Turn left onto Gray's Road.

8.5 Observe the goats grazing on your right.

8.9 Ruins of old barns stand on your side of the road.

9.7 Turn left into the Battle Creek Cypress Swamp and Nature Center.

The sanctuary and nature center are open April through September, Tuesday through Saturday 10 AM–5 PM and Sunday 1 PM–5 PM. During the winter months, the area closes at 4:30. Admission is free. Restrooms and drinking fountains available.

The focal point of the preserve is a nature trail built on a boardwalk over the swamp,

Barns line Calvert County's country roads.

which marks the northernmost stand of bald cypresses in the U.S. Bald cypresses tower as high as a hundred feet overhead, and their feathery deciduous needles form a cathedral-like canopy, sheltering many kinds of birds and splashing filtered light on the swamp below. Watch for turtles and frogs among the sleek knobs that poke through the mud. These knobs are the knees of the trees, an extension of the bald cypress root system. They help brace the trees and may provide oxygen to underwater roots. This really is a special place that, in the words of the promotional brochure, "recalls a time some 100,000 years ago when large parts of Maryland were covered with swamps, and saber-toothed tigers and mammoths roamed the landscape."

After your visit, turn left out of the parking lot onto Grays Road.

10.2 Turn left on Sixes Road, MD 506.

10.3 Sixes Road crosses Battle Creek and climbs a hill.

11.7 The Lyle Simmons House, c. 1920, houses an herb farm (right).

12.0 Sixes Road crosses Adelina Road (MD 508). Continue on Sixes Road, for a refreshing series of downhill glides.

13.8 Cross MD 231 carefully and turn left, riding on the shoulder. Ahead of you, you can see the broad Patuxent River.

16.0 Cross the Patuxent River on a two-lane bridge. Traffic is usually light, so there's no problem riding. There's also a narrow walkway. This is a drawbridge, but it rarely opens.

16.6 On the west side of the river, you enter Charles County.

17.0 Cross MD 231 carefully and enter the town of Benedict, stopping to read the historical marker about the British troops under General Robert Ross landing here in August 1814. When the British arrived, they found a town of small, neat houses, from which the residents had fled. Unbeknownst to the enemy, James Monroe—then an advisor to President Madison—was hiding in the pine forests around Benedict sending intelligence reports to the capital (see also Tour 20). Benedict looks much the same today. Turn left and continue on Benedict Avenue 0.4 mile to The River's Edge Restaurant, which specializes in seafood. If you have parked a car here, this is the end of the trip. If not, it's a good place to refresh for the return trip.

Bicycle Repair Service

4X-Treem Sports, 3865 Old Town Road, Huntingtown, Maryland (410-257-4858)

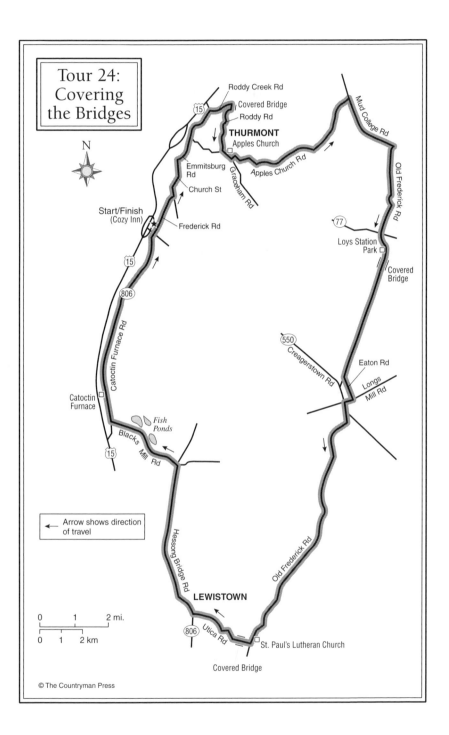

Tour 24:
Covering
the Bridges

N

Roddy Creek Rd
Covered Bridge
Roddy Rd
THURMONT
Apples Church
Mud College Rd

Emmitsburg
Rd
Church St
Apples Church Rd

Start/Finish
(Cozy Inn)
Frederick Rd
Graceham Rd
Old Frederick Rd

15

77

Loys Station
Park

806

Covered
Bridge

Catoctin Furnace Rd

550

Creagerstown Rd

Eaton Rd

Catoctin
Furnace

Longs
Mill Rd

Fish
Ponds

15

Blacks Mill Rd

Arrow shows direction
of travel

Hessong Bridge Rd

Old Frederick Rd

LEWISTOWN

0   1   2 mi.

0   1   2 km

806
Utica Rd
St. Paul's Lutheran Church

Covered Bridge

© The Countryman Press

24

Covering the Bridges

LOCATION: Frederick County, Maryland

TERRAIN: Moderately hilly

ROAD CONDITIONS: Paved country roads with little traffic

DISTANCE: 24.6 miles

HIGHLIGHTS: Three covered bridges, Apples Church, Catoctin Furnace, the Cozy Inn

Covered bridges make perfect sense: since bridge surfaces freeze before solid highways, why not put a roof over them? But modern road planners don't like covered bridges, and the wooden structures, prey to the debilitating effects of time and weather as well as to modernization, are fast disappearing. There were once 52 covered bridges in Maryland. Only 8 remain, and 3 of them are within easy cycling distance of the pleasant town of Thurmont, north of Frederick. All three bridges look exactly alike, constructed of red, beveled German clapboard. But getting to them takes you through pretty farm country where you'll find lots of cows, horses, and pigs to commune with. There are also picturesque towns and inviting streams. The Catoctin Mountains form a dramatic backdrop for the scenery, and you can enjoy them without having to climb them.

The tour begins in the parking lot of the Cozy Inn in Thurmont. To get there, take I-270 north from the Beltway to Frederick. At Frederick, I-270 runs into US 15. Take US 15 north to the Thurmont exit and follow the signs to the Cozy Inn. Tell the reservations clerk you'll be back in about four hours and be sure to come back hungry. The all-you-can-eat buffet is not for the faint of heart.

0.0 Exit the parking lot and turn left onto Frederick Road.

0.3 Just past the community park, turn left onto Church Street.

You are now in the heart of Thurmont, founded in 1751 by a westward-bound family who stopped here with a sick child. They stayed on, started a forge, and other industries grew up to serve the surrounding farms.

0.9 Turn right onto Emmitsburg Road (MD 806), which passes a horse farm and then travels through a small industrial area.

1.9 Turn right onto Roddy Creek Road, which follows Owens Creek through a pleasant wooded area.

2.4 The first and smallest of the three covered bridges, a picturesque barn red, carries you over Owens Creek.

This is a good spot for wading, and the horses in the neighboring field will probably come up to the fence to pose for pictures.

2.4 After crossing the creek, make a sharp right onto Roddy Road, which takes you over rolling hills and past small farms.

3.2 At the intersection with Graceham Road, bear left. Then make the next left onto Apples Church Road.

The stone church (left) that gives the road its name dates from 1826 and was built to serve the German community.

6.1 Make a sharp right onto Mud College Road.

This is a rural road that winds around to the left and has a short gravel stretch.

7.4 Turn right onto Old Frederick Road.

9.1 At Loys Station Park, Old Frederick Road bears right, taking you over the second covered bridge.

This bridge is also made of red, beveled German clapboard and also crosses Owens Creek. There's a swimming hole under the bridge, and just downstream the creek flows over some mini-rapids. This is an ideal picnic spot, with picnic tables but no changing facilities other than a portable toilet. After the park, Old Frederick Road climbs a hill. At the top you'll see a spectacular view of the Catoctins. A little farther on there's a duck pond.

11.2 Turn left onto Eaton Road.

11.6 Turn right onto Longs Mill Road and proceed to the intersection with Creagerstown Road (MD 550). Turn left.

There's a small food store just after the intersection.

11.9 Turn right onto Old Frederick Road, which cuts across some suburban developments.

16.1 St. Paul's Lutheran Church is on a hill to your left. Just past the church, turn right onto Utica Road.

16.4 Another red covered bridge carries Utica Road over Fishing Creek.

The road then winds uphill and down.

17.1 Utica Road ends. Turn right onto Hessong Bridge Road.

18.1 Martin's Grocery, in the village of Lewistown, is on your left.

20.0 Turn left onto Blacks Mill Road, which skirts Little Hunting Creek.

The stream, which invites wading, is on your left. On your right are fish hatchery ponds, but there is no access to them from this road.

21.3 Turn right onto Catoctin Furnace Road (MD 806).

21.8 The ruins on your left are the remains of Catoctin Furnace, which goes back to 1774.

The shells used by the Continental Army at the Battle of Yorktown were made here. The surrounding park has picnic tables. After you pass the furnace, Catoctin Furnace Road veers close to US 15, becoming a frontage road.

23.6 The Blue Mountain Inn (right) is locally famous for its crabs.

After passing the inn, the road descends on Thurmont, running a gamut of fast-food restaurants. Watch for traffic where Catoctin Furnace Road joins Frederick Road.

24.6 Turn left into the Cozy Inn.

Bicycle Repair Service

Frederick Bicycles, 1216 West Patrick Street, Frederick, Maryland (301-663-4452)

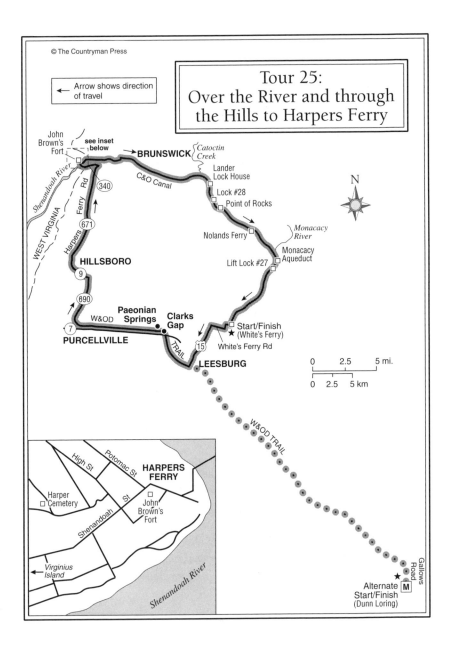

© The Countryman Press

Arrow shows direction
←   of travel

Tour 25:
Over the River and through
the Hills to Harpers Ferry

John
Brown's
Fort

see inset
below

→ **BRUNSWICK**

*Catoctin
Creek*

C&O Canal

Lander
Lock House

Lock #28

Point of Rocks

(340)

Shenandoah River

WEST VIRGINIA

Harpers Ferry Rd

(671)

Nolands Ferry

*Monacacy
River*

HILLSBORO

Lift Lock #27

Monacacy
Aqueduct

(9)

(690)

W&OD

**Paeonian
Springs**

**Clarks
Gap**

(7)

PURCELLVILLE

TRAIL

(15)

Start/Finish
★ (White's Ferry)

White's Ferry Rd

LEESBURG

0	2.5	5 mi.

0	2.5	5 km

W&OD TRAIL

Gallows Road

★

Alternate   M
Start/Finish
(Dunn Loring)

High St

Potomac St

**HARPERS
FERRY**

Harper
Cemetery

St

John
Brown's
Fort

Shenandoah

← *Virginius
Island*

Shenandoah River

25

Over the River and through the Hills to Harpers Ferry

LOCATION: Maryland, Virginia, and West Virginia

METRO ACCESS: Alternate start at Dunn Loring

TERRAIN: A few steep hills in and on the approach to Harpers Ferry; other wise rolling or flat

ROAD CONDITIONS: Two short stretches on heavily traveled highways with wide shoulders; a paved dedicated bike trail; lightly traveled country roads; an unpaved bike trail

DISTANCE: 54 or 102.6 miles

HIGHLIGHTS: A ride on the Jubal A. Early, historic Leesburg, the Washington and Old Dominion Trail, the Breaux Vineyards, the preserved Civil War–era town of Harpers Ferry, the Chesapeake & Ohio Canal

Some say that the Civil War started not at Fort Sumter but at Harpers Ferry, where a fiery abolitionist named John Brown staged a daring raid on the federal arsenal in 1859. (Ironically, the first casualty of the raid was a free black man, commemorated in a memorial erected by the Daughters of the Confederacy.) The raiders were routed by federal troops under the command of Lieutenant Colonel Robert E. Lee. Brown was hanged, but his song went marching on and became a rallying cry for the North.

Harpers Ferry's Lower Town, where this and more took place, is now a National Historical Park with an excellent interpretive program by the National Park Service. Getting there, of course, is more than half the fun of this trip, which begins with a ride on a ferryboat named after another Civil War character, Confederate general Jubal Early. After passing through the beautiful Virginia courthouse town of Leesburg, the trip continues on a rails-to-trails byway, which ends at Purcellville, an antiques mecca. Country roads lead between the hills and down to Harpers Ferry, at the confluence of the Potomac and Shenandoah Rivers. After a respite in one of the town's charming bed & breakfast inns, the return trip crosses the Potomac on a railroad trestle and follows the Chesapeake & Ohio Canal towpath back to White's Ferry.

To reach White's Ferry from the Beltway, take I-270 north to the MD 28 exit and head west to the intersection of MD 107, White's Ferry Road. Turn left onto White's Ferry Road and follow it to the end. There is a large parking lot and a store for stocking up on picnic supplies. The ferry runs seven days a week, year-round, beginning about 6 AM and running till 11 PM except in winter, when it stops at 8 PM. During unusually high water on the Potomac, the ferry may not operate. Call 301-349-5200.

The sole survivor of about a hundred ferries operating on the Potomac, White's Ferry has been in business for about 150 years. General Jubal Early crossed the river hereabouts on his way to raid Washington in 1864 and recrossed shortly thereafter when the raid failed. The boat that is his namesake glides across the Potomac on a cable, and cyclists pay only a small fee.

Note: If you would like a Metro start for this tour, the most convenient one is Dunn Loring, which is 0.7 mile from the W&OD Trail via an on-sidewalk trail. Turn left onto the W&OD Trail and head west. At Leesburg, you will join the main tour. For the return trip, cross the Potomac on the Jubal A. Early and follow the directions to the W&OD Trail at the beginning of the main tour. Turn left onto the W&OD Trail and head east. At Gallows Road, turn right and return to the Dunn Loring Metro station. This will make a round trip of 102.6 miles.

DAY 1

0.0 Ride off the ferry onto the Virginia side and follow the feeder road up a hill, through woods and rolling farmland to the junction with US 15.

1.2 Turn left onto US 15, riding on the shoulder.

3.2 Keep to your right when the road divides, following US 15 Business rather than Bypass.

Near this point, look for a historic marker commemorating the Civil War Battle of Ball's

Bluff, a bloody skirmish that took place in 1861. Union troops were ferried across the canal on barges and many drowned when a boat capsized during the retreat. You are now entering Leesburg, named in honor of Francis Lightfoot Lee, a signer of the Declaration of Independence. US 15 becomes King Street and is lined with shops and restaurants.

4.4 Turn right onto the W&OD Trail.

The trail follows the old roadbed of the Washington and Old Dominion Railroad, whose trains ran from 1859 to 1968. Passengers affectionately called the line "the Virginia Creeper." In 1982, the 45-mile right-of-way was acquired by the Northern Virginia Regional Park Authority, and the paved trail was completed in 1988. It is used by walkers, joggers, in-line skaters, and equestrians as well as cyclists. Watch for horse piles. The trail soon leaves the backyards of Leesburg and wanders through countryside.

8.6 You have now climbed to the highest point on the trail, Clarks Gap. Pass under a hundred-year-old stone arch and cross over VA 7, following the trail signs across the bridge.

9.3 The trail passes through Paeonian Springs.

Eight trains called here every day during the town's heyday—to deliver tourists from Washington who came to savor the cooler air and to "take the waters" at the salubrious spring and to haul gallons of it back home. In 1901, the now almost deserted settlement held three booming hotels.

11.3 The defunct Hamilton Railroad Station stands on your right. Washingtonians escaping the summer heat once disembarked here to cool off in the boardinghouses of this pre–Civil War Quaker settlement.

13.3 The trail seems to end here, but actually it turns left, crosses the VA 7 bypass, and leads into Purcellville. Follow the trail signs.

14.8 The trail ends at the old Purcellville Railroad Station.

Efforts are underway to turn the station into an end-of-trail facility with showers, restrooms, and other amenities. Meanwhile, the town of Purcellville, to your left, offers antiques shops, food stores, and restaurants. Fran's Place, on Main Street, has hearty fare, including excellent milkshakes.

To continue to Harpers Ferry, turn right onto VA 690, which leads out of town and crosses the VA 7 bypass on a bridge.

The road continues through rolling farmland, with spectacular mountain views on your left.

Cyclists cross the Potomac River in the Jubal A. Early.

19.8 At the intersection with VA 9, turn left and follow the road through Hillsboro, whose antebellum stone houses line the road. The market at the Exxon station (left) stocks sandwiches and coffee.

21.8 On your left is Lynfield Farm, a picture-book, white-fenced horse farm.

22.4 At the intersection near a small store, turn right onto VA 671, Harpers Ferry Road.

This road cuts through the hills, with mountain views on both sides and cattle grazing in the foothills.

23.5 Breaux Vineyards (right) is open for tours on weekends.

26.2 St. Paul's Lutheran Church (left), a stone building dating from 1835, has an inviting graveyard.

30.0 After climbing a hill and enjoying a long descent to the river, turn left onto US 340, which has a wide shoulder affording good views of the boulder-strewn Potomac and the gorges on the Maryland side. Follow the bridge across the Shenandoah River into West Virginia.

32.0 Take a sharp right onto Shenandoah Street, the entrance to the lower town area of the historic district.

You will pass Virginius Island, the ruins of a once thriving industrial town drawing power from the Shenandoah River. The street leads directly into the preserved town, where you will find an excellent bookstore and information kiosk. Ask about ranger-led tours.

32.1 At the intersection of Shenandoah and Potomac Streets stands John Brown's Fort, actually the armory fire engine house, where he was captured 36 hours after his raid began.

Lock your bike hereabouts and double back one block along Shenandoah Street to High Street. Go about one block up High Street and turn left onto the town's famous stone steps, which lead past a church used as a field hospital during the Civil War and up to Jefferson Rock. Jefferson is reputed to have stood on this rock and remarked that the view—of the confluence of the Potomac and Shenandoah Rivers—was "worth a voyage across the Altantic." After making your own assessment, follow the path to Harper Cemetery, burial place of Robert Harper, who ran a ferry service here in the mid-1700s.

Most of the bed & breakfasts (see below), as well as the Hilltop House Hotel, are up High Street, a steep climb.

DAY 2

For the return trip, go past John Brown's Fort and walk your bike across the river on the old railroad trestle. When you carry it down the stairs on the Maryland side, you will be on the C&O Canal towpath.

32.5 Turn right onto the towpath.

The canal, completed in 1850 at a total cost of $11 million, helped transport flour, grain, building stone, whiskey, and coal between Cumberland, Maryland, and Georgetown. The mules that pulled the barges walked on this towpath, now a 184-mile hiker-biker trail that runs between the mainly dry canal and the Potomac under a canopy of trees. The trail is unpaved and can be muddy in wet weather. Call 301-739-4200 for trail conditions.

38.0 The towpath passes under the bridge that leads across the river to Virginia.

This bridge is a descendant of one burned by Confederates during the Civil War. The surrounding town, Brunswick, is a busy railroad center.

39.7 Cross Catoctin Creek on Catoctin Aqueduct, a three-arch stone crossing trussed by cables.

41.3 Lander Lock House was home for the tender of Lift Lock #29.

Its 6-foot lift was the smallest on the canal.

44.1 Just past Lock #28, you'll see the town of Point of Rocks.

This is a good place to buy food and view the landmark Queen Anne–style railroad station.

46.0 Stop at Nolands Ferry picnic area.

Like many picnic areas along the towpath, it offers tables, grills, drinking pumps, and portable restrooms.

48.4 The trail crosses the Monacacy River on Monacacy Aqueduct, a 516-foot span consisting of seven arches.

The structure was completed in 1833 and carried the canal across the Monacacy. Look upriver for a view of Sugarloaf Mountain. A pleasant park surrounds the area where the Monacacy runs into the Potomac. After crossing the aqueduct, the towpath curves to the right, following the Potomac.

49.1 A footbridge leads to the lockhouse for Lift Lock #27.

49.2 An electric generating plant lies on your left.

54.0 MD 107 crosses the towpath. Turn right onto this road to the White's Ferry parking lot.

Bicycle Repair Service

Bicycle Outfitters, 19 Catoctin Circle NE, Leesburg, Virginia (703-777-6126)

Bed & Breakfasts

Ranson-Armory House, 690 Washington Street, Harpers Ferry, West Virginia (304-535-2142)

Hilltop House Hotel, 400 East Ridge Road, Harpers Ferry, West Virginia (304-535-2132)

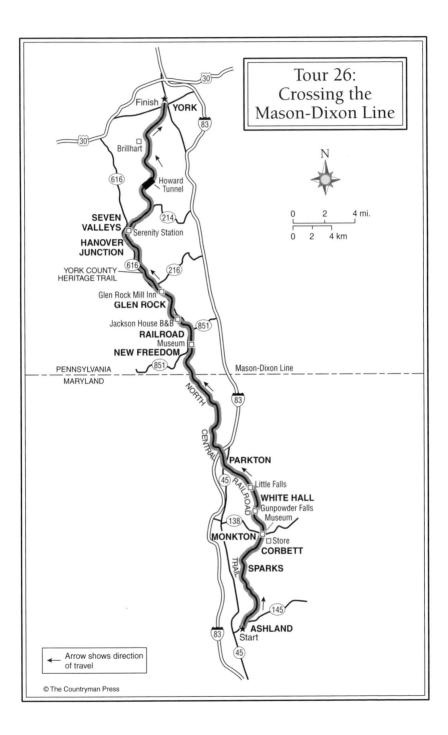

Tour 26:
Crossing the
Mason-Dixon Line

N

0   2   4 mi.

0   2   4 km

Finish
YORK

Brillhart

Howard
Tunnel

SEVEN
VALLEYS
Serenity Station
HANOVER
JUNCTION

YORK COUNTY
HERITAGE TRAIL

Glen Rock Mill Inn
GLEN ROCK

Jackson House B&B
RAILROAD
Museum
NEW FREEDOM

PENNSYLVANIA
MARYLAND

Mason-Dixon Line

NORTH

CENTRAL

PARKTON

RAILROAD

Little Falls
WHITE HALL
Gunpowder Falls
Museum

MONKTON
Store
CORBETT

SPARKS

TRAIL

ASHLAND
Start

← Arrow shows direction
of travel

© The Countryman Press

26

Bonus Trip: Crossing the Mason-Dixon Line

LOCATION: Baltimore County, Maryland, and York County, Pennsylvania

TERRAIN: Flat except for a short uphill climb near the Maryland-Pennsylvania border

ROAD CONDITIONS: Crushed gravel trail

DISTANCE: 41.1 miles one way, or an 82.2-mile round trip

HIGHLIGHTS: Gunpowder Falls, Little Falls, the Monkton Railroad Station and museum, the Mason-Dixon line marker, the New Freedom Station, café, and museum, the old Smyser's Station (now a store that sells ice cream and sandwiches), the Hanover Junction Station and museum, the Howard Tunnel, historic York

This tour follows the route of the North Central Railroad, one of the oldest lines in the United States, which ran from 1838 to 1972 and provided a vital link between the Washington/Baltimore area and Harrisburg, Pennsylvania, upstate New York, and Canada. Built mainly by Irish immigrant laborers, the railroad brought prosperity to area farmers, who shipped milk and produce to urban centers and raw materials to gristmills, sawmills, and woolen mills along the line. During the Civil War, the railroad was targeted by Confederate troops, who cut telegraph lines and destroyed bridges. After the Battle of Gettysburg, Lincoln rode these rails to deliver his famous address, changing trains at Hanover Junction. Later, Lincoln's body traveled this route on the first leg of its journey to its final resting place in Illinois. As railroad use declined, the line fell into disrepair and in 1972, Hurricane Agnes delivered the death blow, washing out bridges.

Maryland converted its section of the line to a hiker-biker trail in 1984, and Pennsylvania followed suit in 1999, but left the tracks intact.

You can start the trip at either end or at several parking lots along the way. This tour begins at the beginning of the Maryland section in Ashland. To get there, take I-83 North from the Baltimore Beltway and exit on Shawan Road (exit 20). Go east 1 mile and turn right on York Road and left on Ashland Road. Continue half a mile to the parking lot.

0.0 Enter the trail and proceed north. The trail crosses a highway and proceeds to the village of Phoenix, where there's another trailside parking lot.

6.2 The trail goes through the village of Corbett, which is on the National Register of Historic Places.
Most of Corbett's dwellings date from 1880 through 1920, the heyday of the railroad, and reflect the village's importance as a commercial and transportation center for the surrounding farms. Unfortunately, the train station was torn down.

6.8 The trail enters Monkton, whose c. 1898 railroad station (left) houses a small museum and visitor center. Across the trail, the Monkton General Store sells sandwiches and drinks. North of Monkton, the river runs beside Gunpowder Falls, a rushing stream that's a popular tubing and canoe route.

10.3 The neoclassical White Hall National Bank dates from 1909. Next to the bank, antique stores coexist with grazing cows and horses. North of White Hall, the trail runs beside Little Falls, whose waters form inviting pools around boulders. Ferns line the banks of both stream and trail, creating a green glade. Paths lead from the trail through the woods to the stream bank.

12.6 The brick building on your right, now a private home, was once an inn for travelers.

15.0 The trail crosses Little Falls and enters a wooded section. There are some road crossings, so observe stop signs.

18.1 As you cross a small stream, look left to see the remains of railroad tracks.

18.5 On your right, Victorian cottages with rockers on front porches face the trail, a reminder of the pretelevision era when watching the train come through was a highlight of the day.

Lincoln changed trains at Hanover Junction on his way to speak at Gettysburg.

19.0 The parking lot for Freeland, Maryland—the last town in this state—is on your left. The tour continues up the only hill on the trip, past restrooms and through woods and farmland.

20.5 A marker indicates the Mason-Dixon Line, the Maryland-Pennsylvania border.

Astronomer Charles Mason and surveyor Jeremiah Dixon drew this line in the 1760s to resolve a property dispute between two of America's first families, the Calverts of Maryland and the Penns of Pennsylvania. When the dispute over slavery heated up nearly a hundred years later, the line took on other significance.

North of the Mason-Dixon Line, the trail is part of the York County Heritage Park. This part of the trail runs beside, rather than in place of, railroad track. The track is not currently in regular use.

21.0 The trail enters New Freedom, its highest point. The restored station (left) houses a café and museum, and a Pennsylvania Railroad caboose sits on the siding.

22.5 The Jackson House Bed & Breakfast and store offers a shaded patio with cold drinks beside the trail in Railroad, Pennsylvania, population 311.

The town has antique stores and a Harley-Davidson factory. The Jackson House was built along the tracks in 1859, when Jackson was a thriving, industrial town, thanks to the railroad. The hotel boasted steam heat and hot and cold running water—a rarity. The stone cistern that held the water still sits on a rise above the house.

After Railroad, the trail passes through a shaded area lined with boulders, jack pine, and mountain laurel, Pennsylvania's state flower.

25.8 The trail passes through the larger town of Glen Rock. The Glen Rock Mill Inn, with a bike rack, sits beside the trail on your right. Built in 1832 as a sawmill, the antique-filled inn now offers food and drink.

North of Glen Rock the trail goes through a long, unshaded stretch.

30.0 The bright red Hanover Junction Station (left) probably looks much as it did on November 18, 1863, when Lincoln changed trains here en route to dedicate a war cemetery in Gettysburg. The restored building houses a Civil War museum, and you can sometimes see re-enactors camped on the lawn.

30.9 Serenity Station—a restaurant, bike rental and repair shop, and wellness center—offers a shaded patio (right).

Built in 1838 as the first store in the village of Seven Valleys, the establishment also served as a train station and post office.

35.7 The trail goes through the 300-foot-long Howard Tunnel, oldest continually used railroad tunnel in the United States. Go slow, as it's dark and damp inside.

Rather than follow the winding path of Codorus Creek, the railroad builders, using mainly Irish immigrant labor, tunneled through a hill with hand drills and black powder. Completed in 1838 and faced with stone in 1840, the tunnel honors Revolutionary War hero Colonel John Eager Howard of Baltimore.

North of the tunnel, the trail runs beside horse farms and country clubs. The area is wooded and shady, with stone cliffs on one side and Codorus Creek on the other. Periodic benches and picnic tables provide resting places.

37.7 In the small settlement of Brillhart, Victorian homes with porches and rocking chairs face the tracks.

39.6 As the trail approaches York, it runs between the creek and old industrial buildings and makes several at-grade crossings.

41.1 The trail ends in a park adjacent to York's Colonial Courthouse in the historic district.

Bicycle Repair Service

Monkton Bike Rental, 1900 Monkton Road, Monkton, Maryland (410-771-4058). Adjacent to trail; rents bikes, tubes, kayaks, and canoes and also does repairs.

Whistle Stop Bike Shop, 2 East Franklin Street, New Freedom, Pennsylvania (717-227-0737)

Serenity Station, 11 Church Street, Seven Valleys, Pennsylvania (717-428-9675)

Accommodations

Jackson House Bed & Breakfast, 6 East Main Street, Railroad, Pennsylvania (717-227-2022)